Praise for *Beyond Me*

"So many Christians I've spoken with recently are weary of me-first spirituality, of self-help sermons and insular ways of 'doing church.' Yet much of modern evangelicalism encourages us to attend to our own spiritual fitness rather than directing the love of God outward, toward others. In *Beyond Me*, Kathi Macias reminds us that as Christ came to serve, so we should also serve. It is a message the church desperately needs to hear."
—**Lynn Vincent**, features editor, *World* magazine, and *New York Times* best-selling coauthor of *Same Kind of Different as Me*

"I love a book that challenges me to think in new ways about my Lord and Savior, Jesus Christ. *Beyond Me* is that kind of book. Kathi Macias has put to amazing use her biblical scholarship, her practical life experiences, and her deft skill as a writer to create a book that expands traditional thinking about the Christian life. If you're not afraid to let your life be radically used by God, you've got to read this book."
—**Peggy Matthews Rose**, coauthor of *Read for Your Life*

"Kathi Macias writes with the conviction of a disciple who lives a life of intimacy with our Creator. Through her words in *Beyond Me*, Kathi accomplishes the mission of proclaiming the truth and equipping readers to become disciples and live out Jesus's call on their lives."
—**Jan Coates**, founder and president, Set Free Today Ministries

"Kathi Macias seizes biblical truth throughout *Beyond Me*. This is a book that can be trusted. With gifted writing and great love for our Lord, she brings Scripture into the challenges of today's world. Fresh insights compel my heart to change."
—**Susan B. Wilson**, president, Executive Strategies

BEYOND

me.

BEYOND

*Living a **You-First** Life in a Me-First World*

By Kathi Macias

New Hope Publishers
Birmingham, Alabama

New Hope® Publishers
P. O. Box 12065
Birmingham, AL 35202-2065
www.newhopepublishers.com

New Hope Publishers is a division of WMU®.

Library of Congress Cataloging-in-Publication Data

Mills-Macias, Kathi, 1948-
  Beyond me : living a you-first life in a me-first world / by Kathi
Macias.
     p. cm.
  ISBN 978-1-59669-220-6 (sc)
  1. Christian life. I. Title.
  BV4501.3.M555 2008
  248.4--dc22
                                        2008004068

Cover designer: Birdsong Creative, Inc. www.birdsongcreative.com

ISBN-10: 1-59669-220-0
ISBN-13: 978-1-59669-220-6

N084143 • 0708 • 7M1

Dedication

To HaShem,
the Name Above All Names,
who has loved me with an everlasting love...
and calls me to walk accordingly.
And to my husband and partner, Al,
who walks this path beside me.

HaShem is Hebrew for the Name
and is often used by Jews to refer to God.

Table of Contents

Foreword

If you are satisfied with your present condition—if you have no yearning to know God better and to serve Him more effectively—then this book might not be suited for you. For those, however, who are looking for new lands to explore, to break away from the humdrum existence that can threaten us all, then read on.

For centuries, the Spanish national motto was *Non plus ultra* (No More Beyond)—affirming the belief that the world was flat and any who ventured beyond were doomed to fall off its edge. Of course, Christopher Columbus later dispelled such notions on his famous voyage of 1492. When the citizens of Valladolid, Spain, eventually erected a monument in the explorer's honor, they paid tribute in a clever way: a statue of a lion sits at the memorial's base, his outstretched paw swiping away the word *Non* from the former motto, leaving the phrase to read simply *Plus Ultra*. So much for national mottoes! In like manner *Beyond Me* beckons us beyond our often self-imposed limitations to venture into a deeper, wider expression of our faith.

Certainly we feel safer remaining on familiar territory. The Lord, however, has not called us to a life of boredom or mediocrity. Borrowing from C. S. Lewis, the Lion of Judah is not one who can be tamed—He is not safe, but He is good. We can trust Him to surround us with His presence as we move into the adventurous role of being one of His disciples. Some believers may be content to have their names recorded in heaven. Disciples, on the other hand, also seek to know the Lord intimately and to serve Him wholeheartedly. Throughout history God has used men and women who would not settle for mediocrity. Many spheres of life—medicine, the judiciary, politics, science, literature, and countless other endeavors—have been pioneered or significantly shaped by Spirit-led disciples of Jesus Christ who sought to serve Him and others with their whole life.

Beyond Me is a clarion call to ever-deepening discipleship. It is an invitation to advance the cause of Christ and to make our lives count. Columbus's journey was not one of ease and simplicity. Storms at sea and a disillusioned crew were among the many trials that beset him. Discovery and advancement often come with such testing, yet the rewards are great.

Kathi Macias invites us to make a difference in the world around us. She compels us to stand and be counted among those who love God with all our heart and who seek to love others ahead of ourselves. She has superbly set the course for those of us who wish to become true disciples of Christ. Kathi makes the way plain and encourages us with practical insights on how we can model a you-first life in a me-first world. There certainly is *more beyond* for all of us, and this worthy book, when acted upon, will help us set sail on an ever-deepening journey with Jesus.

Chris Hayward

Pastor, Author, Speaker
President of Cleansing Stream Ministries

Introduction
Guard Your Heart

Above all else, guard your heart, for it is the wellspring of life.
—Proverbs 4:23 (NIV)

"Greater love has no one than this, than to lay down one's life for his friends."
—John 15:13

G od's Word admonishes us, above all else, to guard our hearts Why? Because the heart is "the wellspring of life." Life flows from a heart that is tender toward God and others; it ceases to flow when the heart is hardened and cares only for self. When we allow ourselves to take what seems to be the easy way— to go with the flow and spend our short time on earth serving only ourselves—our hearts will only grow harder and more self-absorbed. Me-first living mutes our witness to the world and poisons our own lives, reaping only an increase in the ills that plague us: abuse, abandonment, divorce, greed, violence, hatred, stress, fear, immorality, and a general disregard for life at all stages.

This book flows from years of experience trying to guard my own heart. In 1974 I came to know Jesus as my personal Savior, receiving a new and tender heart to replace the heart of stone I'd carried around for 26 years. Since then it has been an ongoing spiritual battle to keep my new heart soft and pliable, open to God's leading instead of following my own desires.

Throughout these three-plus decades in the Lord, I've had the opportunity to serve Him in many capacities, including children's ministry, women's ministry, biblical counseling, prison and homeless ministry, and writing and speaking. But regardless of the season or situation of my life, I've learned that true growth and victory as a believer come only as we guard our hearts and daily lay down our lives for others.

Jesus said, "Greater love has no one than this, than to lay down one's life for his friends" (John 15:13). He also said, "He who finds his life will lose it, and he who loses his life for My sake will find it" (Matthew 10:39). In other words, the Savior is calling us to give away our lives in service to others, preferring them above ourselves so that we might discover a depth of joy found only in selfless living. I must take the focus off me and put it on you—"you" being You, my Lord, and you, my neighbor. Jesus continually taught that such a you-first lifestyle, focused on God and others, *is* possible, if a person has an intimate relationship with Him. The Scriptures, from Genesis to Revelation, stress that same message.

> **This is the definition of the you-first lifestyle: God first, loving Him with all we've got, and then serving our neighbors as ourselves.**

God laid it out about as clear as it can get when He said, "I call heaven and earth as witnesses today against you, that I have set before you life and death, blessing and cursing; therefore *choose life*" (Deuteronomy 30:19, emphasis added). And that's what this book is all about: a call to God's people to respond to His higher purpose for our lives, to guard our hearts against becoming hard and self-centered, to refuse to get caught up in the "me-first" culture of our day, to adopt the selfless cry of John the Baptist: "He must increase, but I must decrease" (John 3:30). This is the definition of the you-first lifestyle: God first, loving Him with all we've got, and then serving our neighbors as ourselves. To put it another way, He is calling us to live a God-and-others-centered life in a self-centered world. Let's heed the very words of the Lord Himself: "Choose life!" For if we, as believers in and followers of Jesus Christ, do not choose to take a stand for life—real life, eternal life—who then is left to stem sin's deadly tide? Who will shine as lights on a hill to the dark world around us?

It is, therefore, up to us, those who have been born again by the very Spirit of God—we who've been given a heart of flesh to replace the "stony heart" described in Ezekiel 11:19—to respond to God's higher calling by daily choosing life over death. We will set the standard by modeling this lifestyle even to those who will hate and persecute us for doing so.

No easy task—and no small one—but necessary nonetheless. More than that, it is a costly calling. Choosing to take a stand for life in the face of a culture of death may very well cost us everything. And yet, it is the very reason we are here on this earth today. Regardless of our station or position in life, our geographic location, our age, gender, talents, or abilities, we are here for one purpose: To answer God's higher call to live beyond ourselves and to model a you-first life in a me-first world. But we can only do that if, first, our stony hearts have been replaced by hearts of flesh through the new birth; and, second, we continually guard our hearts of flesh so they do not begin to harden once again. Hearts of flesh, tender toward God and toward others, are the very wellsprings of life and blessing so desperately needed by a hard-hearted world that walks in darkness under the curse of death—a world of which we were once a part and for which our Savior died.

Will you answer that higher calling to live beyond yourself? Will you accept the challenge to model a you-first life in a me-first world? Will you look with me at what it means to live such a life, a life based on the example of the One who walked the narrow way ahead of us, the road that leads to Calvary and crucifixion, and who now calls to us, "Come, follow Me"?

Again, the cost will be high, but God Himself will walk with us every step of the way, even carrying us when necessary, and when we have arrived at our final destination, we will have the joy of hearing Him say, "Well done, good and faithful servant. Enter into the joy of your Lord." I believe we will also hear the welcoming voices of those whose once hardened, me-first hearts were turned to God when they saw us willingly lay down our lives—not only for our friends, but also for our enemies.

The Price of Love

---

*"But he who is greatest among you shall be your servant.
And whoever exalts himself will be abased, and he who
humbles himself will be exalted."*
—Matthew 23:11–12

As December drew to a close and transitioned into the new year, I found myself spending more and more time alone with God, seeking Him for clear direction for the coming year. When that direction came in the form of a seven-word admonition, it was not at all what I had expected, or hoped, to hear.

Somebody has to set up the chairs.

The first time I heard it, I shook my head, scratched it, and shook it again. Why would God make such a statement, and what did it have to do with me? Surely I had misunderstood. My heart's desire was to write and publish the words He had given me, to speak and teach about His great love and calling for our lives. But the more I tried to convince myself that I had imagined those words—*somebody has to set up the chairs*—the more I knew they had been given to me by the God who says what He means and means what He says.

So I went into the new year believing God wanted me to be content simply helping others with their books and...well, setting up chairs at meetings so others could speak and teach. Without too much resistance, I accepted that and moved ahead—until something happened that caught my attention and clarified my focus.

My 86-year-old mother lives with us. She is a strong Christian and is mentally alert, but her mobility is limited. She's unable to do things most of us do with ease: driving to a doctor's appointment, going to the grocery store, changing the sheets on her bed, standing at the stove to cook a meal. Being her primary caregiver can become stressful and time-consuming, particularly when I'm trying to work all that into an already busy schedule. One day as I rushed around the house, trying to get as much done as possible before running an errand for my mom—all the time wishing I could just sit down at my computer and get some much-needed work done—I caught myself grumbling. Actually I was feeling sorry for myself. And I didn't like the sound of it one bit.

"I'm sorry, Lord," I whispered. "Forgive me for being so selfish and impatient. It's just that I want so much to be working right now."

Somebody has to set up the chairs.

I was stunned. Is that what God had been trying to tell me earlier in the year—that I was in a season of service for my mother, someone who had spent many years of her own life taking care of me?

I felt myself relax as I began to understand God's call to servanthood in my life—my personal call to live a you-first life in a me-first world. It wasn't just about living selflessly so unbelievers would be drawn to Jesus. It was also about daily laying down my life, giving up the right to plan my days and order my steps, so that I could help others fulfill the needs of their day. It was about choosing to honor the sanctity of life, regardless of the personal costs, rather than selfishly guarding the quality and convenience of my life at the expense of others. And I realized that if I allowed a grumbling, complaining, me-first spirit to taint my service to others, including my mom, I was in danger of falling into the grip of the very culture of death I've spent so much time writing and speaking against. I was on the verge of hardening my heart. *Choose life!*

God was calling me to a you-first season of "setting up chairs" for others, especially my dear mother, much as she once did for me. In a similar but much more profound way Jesus did the same for all of us when He walked the lonely road to Calvary and willingly hung on that cross in payment for our sins, giving up His own earthly life so we might gain eternal life. As I pondered the situation with my mother, the question before me was: would I humbly and graciously choose life and blessing . . . or death and curses? His way . . . or mine?

> *God was calling me to a you-first season of "setting up chairs" for others.*

Somebody has to set up the chairs.

If we're honest, we'll admit that we all prefer to be the one on stage, the one receiving the accolades and praise and attention, rather than the silent one in the background, setting up chairs so others can come and rest as they listen to God's message. But if we truly believe we are all one Body, here to serve God and others, then setting up chairs at the women's Bible study is just as vital as giving the keynote address at a national gathering. And caring for those who cannot care for themselves is a great privilege, bestowed upon us by the Creator of the Universe, the Author of Life.

God has not called us to serve ourselves, but to serve others—even to the laying down of our lives if need be. This is the you-first lifestyle in a me-first world. In those selfless acts of love and service, we are serving and honoring God by modeling what He has already done for us. Some may be called to be martyrs of the faith—shedding their blood for Jesus's sake; most of us will simply need to learn how to daily put the needs of others before our own. There is no higher calling, no more fulfilling or joyous existence.

Hearts Hardened Against Truth and Life

Sadly, many in our churches have not discovered the joy of missional living—living a you-first lifestyle in a me-first world.

Their hearts are hardened to God's best for them. And we who have tasted the joys of Christ-first, servant living are easily distracted, frequently returning to our selfish ways and allowing our hearts to harden once again.

Hard hearts are nothing new, of course. Adam hardened his heart against God when he listened to his wife and committed treason in the Garden of Eden. Cain hardened his heart when God rejected his offering; out of that hardened heart, murder entered the world. And hardened hearts have continued to spawn untold pain and suffering down through the ages, as God's command to choose life over death is ignored and curses replace blessings.

Jesus was no stranger to dealing with hard hearts. He never got sidetracked with politics or cultural agendas. He always went straight to the heart of a situation—people's hearts, because He knew that people's actions and words reflect their hearts. He understood that dealing with actions and words is nothing more than a temporary fix. For permanent results, He always dealt with hearts, and He dealt with them one at a time.

Children's hearts are soft and tender, trusting and vulnerable, the very qualities that cause us to want to cherish and protect them.

Going back 2,000 years, we see Jesus, walking the dusty roads of Judea with his 12 disciples and an ever-growing throng of followers, stopping to bless the children. "Unless you are converted and become as little children," He said to His listeners, "you will by no means enter the kingdom of heaven" (Matthew 18:3). What did He mean by that? What was it about His followers that needed to be converted and "become as little children"?

It was their hearts. Children's hearts are soft and tender, trusting and vulnerable, the very qualities that cause us to want to cherish and protect them. But as children get older and begin to learn about the high price of trust and love, as they experience the results of living in a culture that chooses death over life, their hearts change. Protective walls are built, and hardness sets in. Big, round, trusting eyes are replaced with wary glances and suspicious frowns. Joyful, singsong voices give way to sarcastic, cynical words. Mistrust and self-defense override the inner longings for unconditional love and acceptance. Tenderhearted innocence gives way to hardhearted, worldly wisdom.

That is the reason it is often easier to lead young children than adults to Christ. When we present the gospel to children, many readily accept the truth that Jesus loves them, wants to forgive their sins, and come into their hearts. Adults, hardened by time and events, come up with all sorts of reasons not to believe and accept that simple truth:

- How do I know there really is a God?
- If there is a God, how do I know Jesus is the only way to reach Him?
- How can a loving God allow such terrible things to happen in the world?
- Maybe God can forgive some people, but not me. You don't know what I've done! I'm beyond help.
- Who says I'm a sinner? I'm no worse than the next guy. Besides, who decides what's sin and what isn't? After all, it's my life. I should be able to choose what's right for me.

Some of the religious leaders of Jesus's day had their own reasons why they couldn't—or wouldn't—accept Jesus as their Messiah. But all those reasons can be summed up in two words: *hard hearts.*

It is difficult to understand why many of the religious leaders— the very ones who best knew the Scriptures and were supposedly anxiously awaiting the coming Messiah—did not recognize or receive Him when He came. After all, not only did Jesus fulfill the Old Testament prophecies about the Messiah, He also performed miracles that verified His identity.

Many historical and religious sources indicate Jesus wasn't the only one to perform miracles. According to Ron Moseley in his work *Yeshua: A Guide to the Real Jesus and the Original Church,* various first-century rabbis, such as Onias and Hanina ben Dosa, were known for performing miracles of healing and deliverance. However, he goes on to cite scholar Arnold Fruchtenbaum who points out that there were four major types of messianic miracles that ordinary rabbis could not perform: the healing of lepers; the casting out of a demon of dumbness; the healing of someone born blind; the raising of the dead. Jesus performed all four.

The highest religious court of the day, the Sanhedrin, which consisted of 71 members (judges), would routinely send out a delegation to investigate any reports of miracles. The investigation involved two steps: first, observation; second, interrogation. In the early stages of Jesus's miracles, the delegation simply observed Him (see Mark 2:5–7; Luke 5:17); but when He healed the lepers (the first type of the four messianic miracles mentioned above; see Luke 17:11–19), they were forced to consider His claims, and the interrogations began.

Jesus's second messianic miracle was the casting out of a dumb spirit (see Matthew 12:22). Although there were recorded incidences of deliverances by other rabbis, none had ever cast out a demon of dumbness. The reason for this, according to Jewish historians, was that the method the rabbis used to perform a deliverance was to ask the demon its name, and then use the demon's name to cast it out, a method sometimes employed by Jesus (see Mark 5:9). Because a dumb spirit could not speak, the rabbis could not identify it or cast it out. (It was that very type of spirit the disciples could not cast out in Mark 9:17–18.) Jesus was now performing miracles that no one else was able to do, and people were responding with remarks such as, "Could this be the Son of David [the promised Messiah]?" (see Matthew 12:23). Even the members of the Sanhedrin delegation were beginning to take Him seriously.

Then, in the ninth chapter of John, we read of Jesus's healing of a man born blind, another messianic miracle. When the Sanhedrin delegation confronted the man about his healing, he replied, "Since the world began it has been unheard of that anyone opened the eyes of one who was born blind. If this man were not from God, He could do nothing" (vv. 32–33). The delegation was incensed that this man's healing—and now his statements attesting to Jesus's origin—were aiding in the confirmation of the messiahship of Jesus. And so, they "cast him [the healed blind man] out" (v. 34); in other words, they excommunicated him.

Undeniable Evidence

Finally, we come to the famous story of Jesus's raising of Lazarus from the dead (see John 11). Although there are other recorded instances of Jesus raising people from the dead (see Mark 5:21–43; Luke 7:11–17) and even of prophets raising the dead in the Old Testament (see 1 Kings 17:17–24; 2 Kings 4:8–37), the incident with Lazarus is unique. According to Moseley in *Yeshua*, the Pharisees, one of the most influential and respected Jewish sects of Jesus's day, believed that when a person died, the person's spirit hovered over the body for three days; they also believed that during that time there remained an outside chance of resuscitation. However, by the fourth day, all hope was gone.

Along those same lines, the medical technology of that day was not always able to distinguish between someone who was very ill and had slipped into unconsciousness and someone who had actually just died. As a result, people were sometimes buried alive. To guard against such a tragedy, Jewish burial practices incorporated a safeguard. Taken from David Stern's *Jewish New Testament Commentary*, the following quote from an eighth-century Jewish writing outlines that safeguard:

We go out to the cemetery and examine the dead [to see if they are still alive and have been buried by mistake] for a period of three days and do not fear being suspected of engaging in the ways of the Amorites [i.e., superstitious practices]. Once a man who had been buried was examined and found to be alive; he lived for twenty-five years more and then died. Another such person lived and had five children before he died.
—S'machot 8:1

John 11:39 tells us clearly how long Lazarus had been in the grave by the time Jesus got to him: "He has been dead four days." Was it a coincidence that Jesus arrived the day after all Pharisaical hope of resuscitation was gone? Was the delay an oversight on Jesus's part? Was He being uncaring in taking so long to go to His friend's aid? After all, verse 6 tells us, "So, when He [Jesus] heard that he [Lazarus] was sick, He stayed two more days in the place where He was."

Jesus knew exactly what He was doing. He knew the Pharisees' litmus test for proof of messiahship. He also loved these religious leaders and desired that they would recognize and receive Him. So, He willingly ordered His steps in such a way as to fulfill their messianic requirements. In addition, He knew that His disciples, as well as the rest of His followers—nearly all of whom were Jewish—were fully aware of the four messianic miracles and that He had already fulfilled three of them. That is precisely why, when He and His disciples finally set out to go to Lazarus, Jesus announced, "Lazarus is dead. And I am glad for your sakes that I was not there, *that you may believe*" (vv. 14–15, emphasis added). When they arrived, Lazarus "had already been in the tomb four days" (v. 17). For Lazarus and his loved ones, all hope was gone. And then Jesus spoke: "Take away the stone" (v. 39).

Although the stone that sealed Lazarus's tomb had been moved so that life could burst forth, the stony hearts of those particular religious leaders had not been moved at all.

If there were any questions in anyone's mind—any remaining doubt that Jesus was the long-awaited Messiah—the next few moments would settle it once and for all. No one—absolutely no one—had ever raised someone from the dead after four days. Jesus spoke again: "'Lazarus, come forth!' And he who had died came out bound hand and foot with grave clothes, and his face was wrapped with a cloth. Jesus said to them, 'Loose him, and let him go'" (John 11:43–44).

He had passed the Pharisees' litmus test. Jesus had performed every miracle required by the Sanhedrin delegation to prove He was the prophesied Messiah. And so, immediately they bowed down and worshipped Him, right? Wrong. Although the stone that sealed Lazarus's tomb had been moved so that life could burst forth, the stony hearts of those particular religious leaders had not been moved at all. They ignored the command of the very God they claimed to represent: *Choose life!* Instead, verse 53 tells us, "From that day on, they plotted to put Him to death."

Faced with the almost certain fact that Jesus was indeed the Messiah, the religious leaders chose to put to death the One who claimed to be "the way, the truth, and the life" (John 14:6). Despite undeniable evidence of His messiahship, they hardened their hearts even more and chose to reject the One they had been seeking for so very long. Why? Because they had a me-first mentality, and they cared more about preserving their own quality of life than about acknowledging and worshipping the Giver and Sanctifier of all life. The Sadducees, another Jewish sect of Jesus's day, also rejected him. Running the Temple involved great profit and prestige for them, and these men were not ready to give up their comfortable way of life—even to acknowledge and receive the very One for whom the Temple was built, writes Moseley in *Yeshua*. "If we let Him alone like this," they reasoned, "everyone will believe in Him, and the Romans will come and take away both our place and nation" (John 11:48).

And so, Jesus, who had done nothing but offer hope and healing, salvation and restoration, would pay the ultimate price for demonstrating His love: He would lay down His life (see John 15:13).

Jesus died in our place, the perfect, once-and-for-all sacrifice for our sins (see Hebrews 7:26–27). And yet, the very ones who claimed to be looking with longing for His coming rejected Him: "He came to His own, and His own did not receive Him" (John 1:11). They preferred death to life, the curses born out of a hard heart rather than the blessings of a relationship with the living God.

Jesus knew about rejection. He knew about pain and suffering. He knew the price of love, and He willingly paid it. He died in our place that we might live. He chose death so we might choose life. And so, because He suffered and died in our place, paying the ultimate price for love, we should be free from pain and suffering, free to live a materially and physically abundant life, to pursue our own quality of life...shouldn't we? Not if we want to be His disciples.

> *Jesus knew about rejection. He knew about pain and suffering. He knew the price of love, and He willingly paid it.*

Counting the Cost

Discipleship has a price. Jesus said, "A disciple is not above his teacher, nor a servant above his master" (Matthew 10:24). A disciple is a "disciplined one" who follows in the footsteps of his master. A disciple of Christ, therefore, is one who chooses to follow Jesus down the very narrow and difficult way that the Master Himself walked while He was on this earth. Jesus said:

> *"Enter by the narrow gate; for wide is the gate and broad is the way that leads to destruction, and there are many who go in by it. Because narrow is the gate and difficult is the way which leads to life, and there are few who find it."*
> —Matthew 7:13–14

Before believers in Christ were ever referred to as Christians (see Acts 11:26), they were called Nazarenes or "followers of the way." And those early followers quickly learned how narrow and difficult that way was. Many, like Jesus, paid the ultimate price and laid down their lives, considering it an honor and a privilege to do so in His name.

I wonder how many of us today have made that type of commitment. Are we faithfully walking in His footsteps? Or are we more like the Sanhedrin delegation—curious to see Jesus perform miracles, but unwilling to commit to Him? Are we willing to take up His call to be a disciple if it means trading our comfortable lifestyle for a narrow and difficult way that may even include suffering and death?

The only way we can answer those questions is by checking our heart conditions. I can think of nothing more painfully revealing than to ask the Holy Spirit to search my heart, and then to have Him put His finger on a hard place and say, "That has to go. Will you allow me to melt it—or must it be broken?" Ignoring His challenge does not make it go away. Trust me, I know. I've tried to go along my way, refusing to let go of the hard places in my heart, but it just doesn't work.

Public speaking was one of those I'll-do-it-my-way ventures—meaning, I didn't want to do it at all. Even when I knew God was speaking to my heart about launching out into a speaking ministry, I refused to listen. It wasn't until the pain of ignoring Him outweighed my fear of making a fool of myself that I finally said yes to my first speaking invitation. Though I certainly didn't set the world on fire with my oratory skills, I did survive the experience and actually found that it wasn't nearly as bad as I'd expected. My next speaking engagement was less stressful, and I now find that I enjoy public speaking nearly as much as writing. God's way was best for me all along, but until I agreed to turn from my own way and follow His, I missed out on so many blessings just because my heart was hard.

As we saw in the introduction, the heart is the wellspring of life (see Proverbs 4:23 NIV). When we allow our hearts to be hardened, God's life ceases to flow through us as it should. We are useless to the kingdom and to ourselves. So why do we allow the hardness to remain?

Because we, like some members of the Sanhedrin delegation, are afraid of what we may lose—or what we may suffer—if we allow God's Spirit to soften our hearts. Might we lose our comfort, our security, our loved ones, our financial resources, our social standing—our way of life? Will we be hurt, rejected, vilified, ridiculed, and abused, even as He was?

Jesus said:

"Whoever desires to come after Me, let him deny himself, and take up his cross, and follow Me. For whoever desires to save his life will lose it, but whoever loses his life for my sake and the gospel's will save it. For what will it profit a man if he gains the whole world, and loses his own soul? Or what will a man give in exchange for his soul? For whoever is ashamed of Me and My words in this adulterous and sinful generation, of him the Son of Man also will be ashamed when He comes in the glory of His Father with the holy angels."
—Mark 8:34–38

Jim Elliot, who along with four other young missionaries was martyred in 1956 by Huaroni tribesmen in Ecuador, wrote in his journal years earlier: "He is no fool who gives what he cannot keep to gain that which he cannot lose."

> *"He is no fool who gives what he cannot keep to gain that which he cannot lose."*
> *—Jim Elliot*

Jim gave up his earthly life and gained a blessed, joyful eternity with Christ. Although some of the religious leaders of Jesus's day, as well as many of the Jewish common people, accepted Jesus as their Messiah, others did not. Those who rejected Jesus and the eternal life He offered in order to hang on to their temporal way of life were fools. We read the Gospels, and we see it so plainly. And yet, we fail to see that so often we also choose the temporary over the eternal. Why is that?

It is because we have failed to count the cost. Jesus said:

"If anyone comes to Me and does not hate his father and mother, wife and children, brothers and sisters, yes, and his own life also, he cannot be My disciple. And whoever does not bear his cross and come after Me cannot be My disciple. For which of you, intending to build a tower,

does not sit down first and count the cost, whether he has
enough to finish it—lest, after he has laid the foundation,
and is not able to finish, all who see it begin to mock him,
saying, 'This man began to build and was not able to
finish.' Or what king, going to make war against another
king, does not sit down first and consider whether he is
able with ten thousand to meet him who comes against
him with twenty thousand? Or else, while the other is still
a great way off, he sends a delegation and asks conditions
of peace. So likewise, whoever of you does not forsake all
that he has cannot be My disciple."
—Luke 14:26–33

The call to discipleship is serious. The cost is staggering. And
payment is required daily. Understandably, this is a message we
will never hear from a me-first world; but it is less understandable
why we so rarely hear it from the church, especially when we are
first presented with the gospel.

Many of us knelt at a church altar or beside our bed, or prayed
with a friend over lunch, or responded to a television evangelist,
and received Jesus Christ as Savior. It was wonderful, wasn't it?
Nothing equals the joy of discovering the very God of the universe
loves us, sent His Son to die for us, and has made a way to restore
us to fellowship with Himself. The price for salvation has been
paid in full!

But what of the price of discipleship? Jesus didn't tell us to
go into all the world and make converts—He told us to make
disciples:

"All authority has been given to Me in heaven and on
earth. Go therefore and make disciples of all the nations,
baptizing them in the name of the Father and of the Son
and of the Holy Spirit, teaching them to observe all things
that I have commanded you; and lo, I am with you always,
even to the end of the age."
—Matthew 28:18–20

Obviously, we must be converts before we can become disciples; many converts, however, never go on to become disciples. When the initial feelings of joy and excitement begin to wane, some converts sputter out rather than disciplining themselves to pick up their cross and follow the One who saved them, regardless of the cost. They either slide back into their old lifestyle or settle into a sanitized existence, with little change from their pre-conversion days, except that their habits may have been cleaned up a bit and possibly they attend church regularly.

Answering the Call

If I sound as if I'm trying to dissuade people from receiving Jesus as their Savior, I'm not. Nothing moves my heart more than seeing a soul born into the kingdom of God. But I believe we do these new converts a great disservice not to warn them that, though they have chosen the most wonderful and exciting walk imaginable, it is also the most difficult. Continuing to choose life in the midst of an increasingly hostile culture of death will never be easy or popular; therefore, we need to help these new converts learn to count the cost before they set out on the journey.

We need to help these new converts learn to count the cost before they set out on the journey.

For those of us who are already en route, maybe we should reassess our progress. Are we still on target, moving in the right direction, pressing "toward the goal for the prize of the upward call of God in Christ Jesus" (Philippians 3:14)? The only way to be sure is to ask God to perform a heart check. And I warn you ahead of time that it will probably hurt a bit—maybe a lot. But when you think about it, what is the alternative? What happens if we refuse to allow God to do whatever is necessary to keep our hearts soft and tender toward Him?

We could let our hearts turn to stone. We could stop our ears, trying not to hear God's voice. We could refuse to love and be loved. At that point, we might as well hang a sign on our hearts declaring, "Death has won. I will never love—or live—again."

We can deny our need to give and receive love for only so long, for we are all made in the image of God, and God is love (see 1 John 4:8). To deny love is to deny our very purpose for existence.

So what is the answer? How do we protect ourselves from hard hearts in order to answer God's higher calling to choose life—to "deny [yourself], and take up [your] cross, and follow Me" (Mark 8:34)—even when it seems that everyone else is headed in the opposite direction? There is only one way. We must go beyond ourselves and our own finite dreams and abilities, learning to immerse ourselves in God's perfect love. In 1 John 4:18 it is explained this way: "There is no fear in love; but perfect love casts out fear, because fear involves torment. But he who fears has not been made perfect in love."

Perfect love, which comes only from God, can remove our fear and carry us forward into true discipleship. We must make a decision: Will we, out of fear or some other motivation, harden our hearts, as did many of the people of Jesus's day, and cling to what we cannot keep, grasping for a comfortable yet self-seeking life that will end with a sigh—or a scream—at our last breath? Or will we open ourselves to the ongoing possibility of pain and rejection, and like the One who went before us, model a you-first life in a me-first world, offering hope and healing to the lost and dying, even if we must pay the ultimate price?

To willingly lay down our lives in Jesus's name for the sake of others—this is the daily price of love, the sacrificial cost of true discipleship. It is the only offering we can make that will defeat the deadly me-first culture of this world.

Making It Personal

1. What specific issues in today's world most clearly portray the clash between the culture of life and the culture of death? _____

_____

_____

_____

_____

_____

_____

_____

_____

_____

2. What fears or other sinful attitudes keep you from choosing God's way over the world's ways? Life over death? The eternal over the fleeting?_____

_____

_____

_____

_____

_____

_____

_____

_____

_____

_____

_____

3. List your own experiences in which you have had to pay the cost of discipleship. Can you name some instances where Christians, like missionary Jim Elliot and his four young coworkers, have paid the ultimate price?_____

_____

_____

_____

_____

_____

_____

_____

_____

_____

_____

4. Read John 15:13. Write down any instances you can think of in your own life where others showed that kind of love to you, or you showed it to someone else. _____

_____

_____

_____

_____

_____

_____

_____

_____

_____

_____

_____

The Way of Escape

God is faithful, who will not allow you to be tempted beyond what you are able, but with the temptation will also make the way of escape.
—1 Corinthians 10:13

When one of the scribes asked Jesus which is the first, or greatest, commandment in the Law, His answer should not have surprised His audience. His response to the question was to quote from the "Shema Yisrael" portion (see Deuteronomy 6:4–9; 11:13–21) of the synagogue liturgy, which they all knew very well:

"The first of all the commandments is: 'Hear, O Israel, the LORD our God, the LORD is one. And you shall love the LORD your God with all your heart, with all your soul, with all your mind, and with all your strength.' This is the first commandment. And the second, like it, is this: 'You shall love your neighbor as yourself.' There is no other commandment greater than these."
—Mark 12:29–31

Matthew relates the same incident, quoting Jesus as Mark has, but adding these key words: "On these two commandments hang all the Law and the Prophets" (Matthew 22:40).

Jesus answered this scribe's question by citing the central affirmation of Judaism, which is also a central affirmation of Christianity. Jesus was saying that if we seek to fulfill these two commandments, we will be fulfilling the others as well. This is precisely what He meant when He said, "If you love Me, keep My commandments" (John 14:15).

The first time I came across John 14:15 I was a new believer in my mid-20s, and it struck me as a very threatening Scripture. I read it as, "If you *really* love Me as you say you do, *prove it* by keeping My rules!" How inadequate I felt to prove my love, for I knew from past experience how fallible and inept I was at keeping rules.

Without the benefit of a Christian home, I had acquired just enough knowledge about God to make me dangerous—and miserable. I can't remember a time in my life when I didn't believe that God existed and that He was omniscient, omnipresent, and omnipotent. None of that was a comfort to me, however, because I also believed He would someday scrutinize my life—hanging the good and the bad in the balance—and I would be found seriously wanting. Hell loomed ominously on the horizon.

> *Without the benefit of a Christian home, I had acquired just enough knowledge about God to make me dangerous—and miserable.*

And so I went to church with friends and neighbors whenever I had the chance, hoping to find an answer to my dilemma. As a result, I managed to amass a smattering of Catholic, Baptist, Lutheran, and Pentecostal teachings by the time I reached my teens, even living for a time in a Catholic convent. But when, at the age of 15, I left the convent after four months, all the hours I had logged in penance and prayer, fasting and meditation, served only to reinforce my anticipation of eternal doom.

In fact, it was an incident that took place at the end of my stay in the convent that finally erased any last hope for heaven I still had hidden in the deepest recesses of my heart. Having been in the convent for a few months, I had become quite familiar with the religious routines, to the point that much of the bowing, breast-beating, kneeling, and genuflecting had become automatic. But one Sunday afternoon, as I entered the chapel for Benediction, in the midst of the burning incense and the Latin chants of the priest, I suddenly wondered, *Why do we genuflect on one knee for Mass, but two for Benediction?* I understood that the word *benediction* meant blessing, but beyond that I had no real understanding of this Sunday afternoon ceremony.

I noticed one of the nuns on her knees, reciting her rosary, so I knelt beside her and whispered my question. She was a bit annoyed at having her prayers interrupted and answered me in a hushed, impatient tone: "We genuflect on two knees at Benediction because Christ is present on the altar. That's what makes it a special blessing."

Her answer cut me like a knife—not because her words were curt and clipped, but because I believed them to be true. If Jesus Christ—whom I fully acknowledged as the holy, sinless Son of God—was truly there on the altar, I understood full well that genuflecting on two knees was not enough to make me worthy of being in His presence. In fact, I knew at that moment that if I threw myself on my face, it would not be enough. With the heartbreaking realization that there was nothing I could do to make myself worthy to come into His holy presence, I got up and walked out of that chapel and scarcely set foot in church again for 11 years.

Ambushed!

In my 15-year-old mind, my fate was sealed. And so, I decided to do my own thing. After all, if the only future I had was hell, I might as well enjoy life while I could. But on Friday, July 5, 1974, at the age of 26, with my personal life in a shambles and doing-my-own-thing looking less and less attractive by the moment, everything changed when, in the words of author Brennan Manning in *Abba's Child,* "I was ambushed by Jesus of Nazareth."

I was living in Colorado Springs at the time. My parents had moved from California to southwestern Washington when my father retired in 1973. In the years preceding their move, some major changes had taken place in my family.

My younger brother, Bob, had become a Christian in 1969 and had gone off to Bible college. In 1971, my mother was born again at the age of 50. Then, just before my parents' move to the Pacific Northwest, my youngest brother, Jerry, also received the Lord. Needless to say, by this time they were all praying in earnest for yours truly. (My father too was not a Christian at this time. For more on my family's story and how to become a Christian, see the appendix, "Dad and Me.")

> *Before I could get two words out of my mouth, she said, "You need Jesus."*

On the morning of July 2, 1974, my mother's 53rd birthday, she awoke to hear the Lord whisper to her heart, "I have a special gift for you." She knew immediately that it was my salvation. And so, she, along with two faithful friends from her church, began to bombard heaven on my behalf.

I was hundreds of miles away, totally unaware of their intercession but feeling the effects of their warring in the heavenlies. For three days it seemed as if I were literally being torn in half. Part of me wanted desperately to escape the downward spiral of my disintegrating personal life; the other part of me maintained a rebellious desire to do my own thing.

On that hot July 5 afternoon, I could stand it no longer. I called my mother for advice, and maybe a bit of sympathy. Before I could get two words out of my mouth, she said, "You need Jesus." She said a lot of other things to me that afternoon (and prayed for me over the phone), but I really don't remember any of it. The only words that echoed in my mind as I hung up that receiver were "You need Jesus"—that, and her admonition to "Promise me you'll pray when you get off the phone."

I promised I would, but, as soon as I hung up I felt so dirty that I immediately went into the bathroom and took a shower. But no matter how much I scrubbed, I couldn't seem to get clean.

That's when I realized I wasn't dirty on the outside—I was dirty on the inside. I jumped out of the shower, threw on some clothes, and hurried into the bedroom, where I knelt down beside the bed and began to pray. I had no idea what to say, except, *"God, I'm sick of my life the way it is. I've made a mess of it, and I don't want to continue this way anymore. Please help me!"*

That's when He brought to my memory that day in the convent chapel when I realized there was nothing I could do to make myself worthy to come into His holy presence. And then He showed me something amazing. I saw myself standing on a dusty road, a loud and boisterous crowd around me—some weeping, some jeering, some screaming—jostling me as I craned my neck to see what they were looking at. I strained my eyes to see—and then He came into view: Jesus, beaten, bruised, and bloody, was stumbling toward me, carrying His cross.

As I stared, horrified, I could see the agony on His face, and it broke my heart. I began to cry as He drew closer. And then, as He drew even to where I stood amidst the screaming crowd of onlookers, He stopped. Turning His head and looking straight into my eyes, the pain on His face was overshadowed by a tender look of compassion, as He spoke five words that changed my life forever: "I did it for you."

And suddenly I understood. Jesus hadn't just died on the cross for the sins of the world—He had died for me, for my sins! The very thing I had realized 11 years earlier that I was helpless to do for myself, He had already done for me.

> *I had finally found the way of escape from hell. That way—the only way—is Jesus.*

Oh, the waves of joy that swept over me, as I knelt there, weeping and laughing simultaneously. The terrifying surety of an eternity in hell had just been washed away by the revelation of what Jesus had done—*for me*! I had finally found the way of escape from hell. That way—the only way—is Jesus.

Amazing grace, how sweet the sound! And I had heard it in the voice of my Savior: "I did it for you." There wasn't a doubt in my mind that the joy I felt at that moment would stay with me forever.

O, Foolish Galatian!

I was wrong. Within a few years, I'd exchanged joy for exhaustion. Having thrown myself into Bible study, church attendance, and serving God, I soon found myself in a place where I was no longer amazed by grace. Instead, I had become a twentieth-century Galatian, "bewitched" into believing that what God had begun in the Spirit, I could somehow finish in the flesh. I had lost sight of the lesson Jesus had so clearly imparted to me that afternoon when I received Him as my Savior.

> *O foolish Galatians! Who has bewitched you that you should not obey the truth, before whose eyes Jesus Christ was clearly portrayed among you as crucified? This only I want to learn from you: Did you receive the Spirit by the works of the law, or by the hearing of faith? Are you so foolish? Having begun in the Spirit, are you now being made perfect by the flesh?*
> —Galatians 3:1–3

How could I have forgotten so quickly that there was absolutely nothing I could *do* to make myself worthy of being in His presence? I suppose I got so busy trying to do good things and prove my love that I failed to keep focused on the fact that He had already accomplished all that needed to be done—and He had done it for me.

But isn't that a common trap into which many of us Christians fall? I believe it is. In fact, I believe more Christians have been sidetracked by trying to *do* Christianity—instead of just *being* a grateful child of God—than have fallen into the trap of blatant, carnal sin. As a result, a dying world sees little in our lives to convince them to join us.

True, we should never feel so confident in our walk with God that we imagine ourselves immune to destructive, obvious sins like stealing or adultery or murder. But a much greater danger lies in failing to observe the warning in Proverbs 4:23: "Above all else, guard your heart, for it is the wellspring of life" (NIV).

It is when we fail to guard our hearts against becoming hardened toward God (and our fellow man) that we forget about *being* and become obsessed with *doing*. We no longer take the time to gaze into His loving face or listen to His reassuring words, and we

In fact, I believe more Christians have been sidetracked by trying to do Christianity—instead of just being a grateful child of God—than have fallen into the trap of blatant, carnal sin.

somehow—foolishly—come to believe that we can walk in His footsteps without holding His hand. And then, with an ever-hardening heart, we expend more and more energy trying to *do* religion, just as did many of the people of Jesus's day, those who ultimately rejected Him as their Messiah. Aren't we then standing on the same faulty foundation on which they stood, as they foolishly failed to grasp what they potentially could not lose in a futile effort to hold on to that which they could not keep?

In an effort to prevent us from ending up on that faulty foundation, the Apostle Paul reminds us in 1 Corinthians 3:10–11 of the only true foundation on which to build our faith:

> *According to the grace of God which was given to me, as a wise master builder I have laid the foundation, and another builds on it. But let each one take heed how he builds on it. For no other foundation can anyone lay than that which is laid, which is Jesus Christ.*

What happens when we try to stand on a faulty foundation? We fall. Sooner or later, the earth quakes, our faulty foundation crumbles, and we find ourselves lying on our face in the dirt. And we wonder, *What happened? How did I get here? Where did I go wrong?*

Foundations Are Crucial

Jesus told an interesting story about foundations. It's found in Matthew 7:24–27:

> *"Therefore whoever hears these sayings of Mine, and does them, I will liken him to a wise man who built his house on the rock: and the rain descended, the floods came, and the winds blew and beat on that house; and it did not fall, for it was founded on the rock. But everyone who hears these sayings of Mine, and does not do them, will be like a foolish man who built his house on the sand: and the rain descended, the floods came, and the winds blew and beat on that house; and it fell. And great was its fall."*

"Whoever hears these sayings of Mine, and does them..." What "sayings" is Jesus talking about here? And how are we supposed to do them? Jesus begins this story of the wise man and the foolish man with the word *therefore*. This is always a clue to go back and see what went before, as *therefore* ties the two sections together. So just what was Jesus talking about before He told this story?

He was stressing the importance of truly knowing Him— not knowing *about* Him, and not even having had a nodding acquaintance with Him at some point in time. The implication is that we need to know Him in an intimate, ongoing way if we want to live with the assurance that we will spend eternity basking in His presence.

> *"Not everyone who says to Me, 'Lord, Lord,' shall enter the kingdom of heaven, but he who does the will of My Father in heaven. Many will say to Me in that day, 'Lord, Lord, have we not prophesied in Your name, cast out demons in*

*Your name, and done many wonders in Your name?' And
then I will declare to them, 'I never knew you; depart from
Me, you who practice lawlessness!'"*
—Matthew 7:21–23

For someone like me, who felt threatened by John 14:15—"If
you love Me, keep My commandments"—it was easy to misread
the above passage of Scripture as, "Depart from me, you who
do not obey my commandments!" But was the breaking of the
commandments the reason Jesus declared, "Depart from Me"?
No. It was lack of relationship. "I never knew you," He said,
and then referred to those being sent away as "you who practice
lawlessness."

How do you *practice* lawlessness? And just what sort of
lawlessness did Jesus have in mind? First of all, when you practice
something you rehearse it, you repeat it, you continue in it until
it becomes a way of life. To practice
lawlessness, one would have to
continue in that lawlessness until it
became a lifestyle. So does that mean
those who practice lawlessness are
those who continually break the Ten
Commandments? Certainly those
who day in and day out practice evil
lifestyles, like those Paul mentions in
1 Corinthians 6:9–10 for instance,
and who never repent and turn
to God, are indeed lawless. But I

> *If we are cultivating
> an ongoing love
> relationship with God,
> living a life that has
> an ever-growing
> passion for Jesus at
> its center, then our
> lives will be marked
> by obedience to His
> commands.*

believe Jesus was addressing a much deeper issue of lawlessness,
the very form of lawlessness out of which every other act of
lawlessness flows: lack of relationship with and love for the great
Lawmaker Himself.

Let's look back at what Jesus said about the first and second
greatest commandments: "'You shall love the LORD your God with
all your heart, with all your soul, with all your mind, and with
all your strength.' . . . 'You shall love your neighbor as yourself'"

(Mark 12:30–31). He added: "On these two commandments hang all the Law and the Prophets" (Matthew 22:40).

Jesus says that to have a right relationship with God, to be assured eternal life in His kingdom, we need to be in love with Him. If we do not love Him with all our heart, mind, soul, and strength—if we do not treasure Him and put Him first in our lives—then we are practicing lawlessness. We might be doing all the right religious things (see Matthew 7:22, miracles and wonders even), but if He doesn't know us and we don't know Him in an intimate way, we are practicing lawlessness.

However, if we are cultivating an ongoing love relationship with God, living a life that has an ever-growing passion for Jesus at its center, then our lives will be marked by obedience to His commands. I believe that's what Jesus meant when He said, "On these two commandments hang all the Law and the Prophets" (Matthew 22:40). It is also what He meant in John 14:15 when He said, "If you love Me, keep My commandments." Contrary to what I had always thought, John 14:15 is not a threat—it's a promise! What an incredible release I experienced in my Christian walk when I finally stumbled across this great truth.

Crushed

One day when I was feeling tired of all my *doing*, the Lord led me to the book of Ezekiel, where He describes His feelings toward those who were unfaithful to Him: "I was crushed by their adulterous heart which has departed from Me" (Ezekiel 6:9).

> *The words seemed to jump off the page as I read them again and again. "I was crushed," God said. Crushed!*

The words seemed to jump off the page as I read them again and again. "I was crushed," God said. Crushed! Not just hurt or saddened, but crushed. I was shocked and amazed. Why hadn't I ever realized the extent of pain that we, as unfaithful children, can inflict on our heavenly Father? Maybe it was because I had always thought of myself as too insignificant to be able to have such an effect on *El Shaddai*, the Almighty God. Or maybe I hadn't realized it because I was too caught up in what I was doing *for* God to understand what I was doing *to* Him.

Whatever the reason, the Lord allowed that realization to break the hard places in my heart and to open my spiritual eyes to the truth He wanted to emblazon on the very core of my being forever: "Your sin was not so much in the things you did, nor was it in loving other things or other people too much. *Your sin was in not loving Me enough.*"

Once again, I found myself in tears, not only as I digested the impact of God's indictment, but also as I remembered the words He had spoken to me years earlier: "I did it for you." How could I so carelessly and callously have left my first Love? How could I have gotten so caught up in "doing" that I had slipped away from that precious intimacy of continual communion with the Lover of my soul?

During the days and weeks that followed, I meditated on these things. And one day I came across two quotes that deepened my understanding of God's words to me and quickened my resolve to remain safely in His arms:

> *God does more by His Word alone than you and I and all the world by our united strength. God lays hold upon the heart; and when the heart is taken, all is won.*
> —Martin Luther

> *Love for God is ecstatic, making us go out from ourselves: it does not allow the lover to belong any more to himself, but he belongs only to the Beloved.*
> —St. Dionysius the Areopagite

This time God had truly broken through and laid hold upon my heart, and now I belonged only to Him. Where once I had loved Him out of gratitude for what He had done for me, I now loved Him *because He is God*. Although I'd been a Christian for several years already, I only then understood why Jesus said that loving God with all our heart, soul, mind, and strength is the first and greatest commandment. I no longer felt threatened by Jesus's words in John 14:15: "If you love Me, keep my commandments." Keeping His commandments had suddenly become simple and joyful, because I knew that to do otherwise would leave His great and gracious heart "crushed." My love for Him had become too strong and passionate to risk that happening again.

The True Foundation

God had exposed my faulty foundation and lovingly placed me back on the Rock, the only foundation upon which anything solid and lasting can be built. As a result, I understood what the Apostle Paul meant when he said in 1 Corinthians 10:13, "God is faithful, who will not allow you to be tempted beyond what you are able, but with the temptation will also make *the way of escape*" (emphasis added). The key to finding God's promised way of escape is to go back to the preceding verse where Paul says, "Therefore let him who thinks he stands take heed lest he fall" (1 Corinthians 10:12).

> *I got sidetracked trying to prove my love by doing right things and not doing wrong things.*

I thought I was standing—and I was but not on the right foundation. When Jesus had revealed Himself to me as the One who had already done for me all that was necessary to restore my relationship to God, I started out on the right foundation. But I didn't stay there. I got sidetracked trying to prove my love by doing right things and not doing wrong things. In the process, I strayed away from my first Love and ended up on the wrong foundation, just as some of the Jewish people had done so many years before. And like them, I was destined to fall.

At the beginning of 1 Corinthians 10:12 we see that pivotal word *therefore*. Looking at the preceding verses, we see a reminder of how many of the Jewish people, so freshly and miraculously liberated from bondage in Egypt, lost sight of their Deliverer and began to focus on themselves. In other words, they had a me-first mind-set. As a result, every imaginable sin followed, including idolatry, fornication, grumbling, and unbelief, each rooted in the Israelites' lack of love for, and lack of gratitude to, their great God. After reviewing these sins and their devastating consequences, Paul writes, "Now all these things happened to them as examples, and they were written for our admonition.... *Therefore* let him who thinks he stands take heed lest he fall" (1 Corinthians 10:11–12, emphasis added).

The unfaithfulness of the Israelites serves as a warning to us. They thought they were standing—after all, weren't they God's chosen people, redeemed by His mighty hand? Likewise, don't we, having been redeemed by God's mighty hand, oftentimes think we are standing, only to find ourselves face down in the mud? Is our fall unusual?

Of course not. In fact, the first part of 1 Corinthians 10:13 makes that very clear:

*No temptation has overtaken you except such as is common to man; but **God is faithful**, who will not allow you to be tempted beyond what you are able, but with the temptation will also make **the way of escape**, that you may be able to bear it (emphasis added).*

We will never face anything in this life that has not been faced by others before us. And what does God expect us to do when the temptation comes? Submit ourselves to Him. The Scripture does not say that *we* are faithful; it says "*God* is faithful," and He is the One who makes "the way of escape." The only thing we can do in the face of temptation is to

> *We will never face anything in this life that has not been faced by others before us. And what does God expect us to do when the temptation comes? Submit ourselves to Him.*

stay on the right foundation by hanging on to the One who is faithful. To do otherwise is to give in to the very temptation that is at the root of every other temptation we face: the temptation to abandon God's way and revert to our own.

But if we have not already cultivated an ongoing, intimate love-relationship with Him, then when the temptation to abandon God and depend on ourselves comes—and it will—it is unlikely that we will be able to remain standing. Instead, we will revert to our old ways, as did the Israelites, and try to do something on our own to remedy the situation. In other words, we will attempt to create our own way of escape, and as a result we will fall.

We do not prove or disprove our love to God by our own feeble attempts to keep His commands and teachings. God knew from the beginning that we would never be able to do that. That's why He set up the sacrificial system for the Israelites, and that's why He sent His Son to be the ultimate Sacrifice for all of our sins. He took care of the sin problem for us. Out of love and gratitude for what He has already done and for who He is, we then begin to walk in love and obedience to Him.

> The root of
> our sin lies
> in the weakness
> of our love for Him,
> in abandoning
> His way and
> going our own.

It sounds simple, doesn't it? But if we are not standing on the right foundation—"For no other foundation can anyone lay than that which is laid, which is Jesus Christ" (1 Corinthians 3:11)—we will not be able to appropriate His way of escape, because we will be too busy trying to create our own. A fall is inevitable.

The root of our sin lies in the weakness of our love for Him, in abandoning His way and going our own. We must, therefore, resolve to guard our hearts against becoming hardened toward Him, and thereby straying from the only firm foundation.

On July 5, 1974, God showed me "the way of escape" from hell. Later He showed me "the way of escape" from self and that is to do as Jesus admonished us: "Love the LORD your God with all your heart, with all your soul, with all your mind, and with all your strength." There simply is no other foundation from which to begin modeling a you-first life in a me-first world. If we don't start with a consuming love for God, then our service to others will not honor Him and will likely end in frustration and ineffectiveness.

Making It Personal

1. Describe any personal tension you've experienced between loving and obeying God._____

_____

_____

_____

_____

_____

_____

_____

_____

_____

_____

2. How does it make you feel to consider that your own wanderings can cause the very heart of God to feel crushed? _____

_____

_____

_____

_____

_____

_____

_____

_____

_____

_____

_____

3. List some times when you have been so caught up in doing things for God that you were too busy to spend time in His presence, communing with and cultivating your love relationship with Him. _____

_____

_____

_____

_____

_____

_____

_____

_____

_____

_____

4. Read 1 Corinthians 10:13. Try to memorize it. Can you list some times in your life when God has shown Himself faithful by providing a way of escape from a dilemma or problem? How did it make you feel when you realized that God had stepped in to rescue you? _____

_____

_____

_____

_____

_____

_____

_____

_____

_____

_____

_____

3

Do unto Others

"Therefore, whatever you want men to do to you, do also to them, for this is the Law and the Prophets."
—Matthew 7:12

Before I became a Christian, I found that one of the first questions people would ask me at a party or gathering was, "What's your sign?" They were, of course, referring to astrological signs, seeking to find out which sign I was born under so they might better understand what makes me tick. To some degree I found that interesting, but for the most part I found it annoying to be pigeonholed.

Once I came to believe in Jesus as my Savior, I began to move in somewhat different social circles, where the question was no longer "What's your sign?" but "What's your ministry?" To be perfectly honest, I found that question even more disturbing than the one that had been posed to me by unbelievers. I suppose that was because I didn't have a clue how to answer it. Yet so many others in Christendom seemed to know where they fit; why didn't I?

In seeking out the advice of more mature Christians, I was told, "Don't worry about it. God has a place for you. Just try different things, and you'll know when you find the ministry that's right for you."

And so, I did just that. I spent time in the nursery and with the toddlers; I tried my hand at working with teens; I became involved with jail ministry and working with the homeless, as well as alcoholics and drug addicts; I led Bible studies and taught Sunday school and leadership training classes; I wrote devotionals, poems, short stories, and books; I even served for a while as a biblical counselor at a large southern California church. Some of these endeavors I enjoyed more than others; some seemed to produce more positive results than others; some, including writing and teaching, I continue to be involved in to this day; but none seemed to be the one and only slot with my name on it.

Why is that? Why do some people seem so confident in the knowledge that their ministry is working with children or visiting people in hospitals or singing in the choir, while others of us feel backed into a corner when someone asks, "What's your ministry?"

After many years of praying about and studying this issue, I have come to believe this uneasiness stems from ignorance regarding the ministry that has been assigned to *all* believers. At least, I know that was true in my case. Things began to clear up for me one day as I was reading through a familiar passage of Scripture:

For the love of Christ compels us, because we judge thus: that if One died for all, then all died; and He died for all, that those who live should live no longer for themselves, but for Him who died for them and rose again.... Now all things are of God, who has reconciled us to Himself through Jesus Christ, and has given us **the ministry of reconciliation**, *that is, that God was in Christ reconciling the world to Himself, not imputing their trespasses to them, and has committed to us* **the word of reconciliation**. *Now then, we are ambassadors for Christ, as though God were pleading through us: we implore you on Christ's behalf,* **be reconciled to God**.
—2 Corinthians 5:14–15,18–20 (emphasis added)

Did you notice those highlighted words? *The ministry of reconciliation. The word of reconciliation. Be reconciled to God.*

Our ministry is not simply working in the nursery or singing in the choir or visiting the sick. Our ministry is the *ministry of reconciliation*! Jesus was in the world, reconciling people to God, calling them out of death and into life. But now He has gone back to sit at the right hand of the Father and to await His Father's command to return for His bride. And while He is gone, what are we—His bride—to be doing with our time? We are to be

Everything we do must be centered in the ministry of reconciliation, calling people from death to life, and we must understand it is His ministry and not ours.

continuing the ministry of reconciliation that Jesus began while He was here, calling people out of the culture of death into the assurance of eternal life. Ultimately, it remains His ministry and His work; we are simply privileged to participate in it.

Now I realize that our part in His ministry of reconciliation will manifest in different ways in each of us. For some it may very well be working in the nursery or singing in the choir or visiting the sick. For others it may be writing or teaching. But for *all* of us, everything we do must be centered in the ministry of reconciliation, calling people from death to life, and we must understand it is His ministry and not ours. Without that clear understanding and corresponding behavior, we will not be faithful ambassadors who are fulfilling the task that has been committed to us. Nor will we be walking in the you-first life of Christ.

All of our ministry takes place in the context of relationship. As the saying goes, there are no Lone Ranger Christians. We are a body of believers, interconnected with and interdependent on one another, so that we may fulfill Jesus's ministry of reconciliation. As we begin to understand the connection between reconciliation and relationship, we also begin to understand how God has gifted and equipped each of us individually to carry out our part in this awesome ministry that has been entrusted to us.

People who are not yet reconciled to God and to His people are, whether they realize it or not, looking for a way to connect, a way to develop and sustain healthy, fulfilling relationships. Questions like "What's your sign?" and "Haven't we met somewhere before?" are nothing more than futile, impotent attempts to do just that. And yet, those very questions can be an opportunity for us as Christians to address the searching and need in their lives. We simply have to allow ourselves to be compelled by the love of Christ to step into those openings and risk whatever results may come our way. Sadly, that's where the process most often breaks down.

Who Is My Neighbor?

Most of us have read the story of the good Samaritan (see Luke 10:25–37). This section of Scripture starts out with a lawyer testing Jesus, "What shall I do to inherit eternal life?" Jesus tosses the question right back in the lap of this legal expert by asking: "What is written in the law? What is your reading of it?"

The man answers with a quote taken directly from the Scriptures: "'You shall love the LORD your God with all your heart, with all your soul, with all your strength, and with all your mind,' and, 'your neighbor as yourself'" (Luke 10:27). Jesus commends him on answering correctly, and then adds, "Do this and you will live" (v. 28). Immediately the lawyer tries to "justify himself" by looking for some loophole: "And who is my neighbor?" (v. 29).

Of course, Jesus responds by telling the parable of the good Samaritan, a story familiar and comforting to us today but shocking to the original listeners. (Read Luke 10:30-35.) Jesus concludes by asking the lawyer a final question of his own:

> *"So which of these three do you think was neighbor to him who fell among the thieves?"*
> *And he said, "He who showed mercy on him." Then Jesus said to him, "Go and do likewise."*
> —Luke 10:36–37

Go and *do* likewise. Ultimately that was Jesus's answer to the lawyer's question, "What shall I *do* to inherit eternal life?" But what exactly was Jesus saying here? Go and *do what* likewise?

First of all, let's look at the players in this particular story. Who was the story about? It was about "a certain man who went down from Jerusalem to Jericho." Now, since Jesus didn't label this man as a Gentile or a Samaritan, he was undoubtedly a Jew, someone with whom this lawyer could identify—which, of course, was Jesus's intent. And, more than likely, this man from Jerusalem was a man of substantial financial means, since he was targeted by thieves. So not only did the legal expert now identify with the man as a fellow Jew, but he respected him because of his financial position.

Next, we see this Jewish businessman beaten, robbed, and left for dead. Surely this aroused some feeling of empathy within the lawyer. But what happens next? A priest—a highly respected religious leader—comes along and sees the man lying on the opposite side of the road. What would be the anticipated response? The priest would stop and help him, of course. But he doesn't. He leaves him lying there, not even bothering to cross to the other side of the road to see if the man is still alive. Likewise, another religious leader—a Levite—comes along and reacts in exactly the same manner as the priest who has gone before him. Why? Was it nothing more than indifference that caused these two religious leaders to pass by the seriously injured man?

> *Was it nothing more than indifference that caused these two religious leaders to pass by the seriously injured man?*

Although Jesus didn't elaborate on these two religious leaders, they may have been Sadducees. In contrast, the lawyer questioning Jesus was probably a Pharisee, simply because the majority of the people who followed and conversed with Jesus were Pharisees or at least more oriented toward the Pharisees' way of thinking. This is an important distinction when considering the two religious leaders' reactions to the injured man in Jesus's parable. According to the written law, the *Torah*, priests and Levites were forbidden to touch a dead person (see Leviticus 21:1; 22:4). However, the oral law—which Brad Young in *The Parables* defines as the "oral interpretation of the *Torah* that flourished within the broader movement of Jewish theological reflection and that characterized the discussions of the Pharisees"—stressed the sanctity of human life. Young writes, "In Jewish oral tradition, the principle of saving life at all costs gained unsurpassed and uncompromised priority.... All written laws of the *Torah* must be violated to preserve life."

So, according to oral tradition, even if the robbery victim appeared dead, the priest and Levite should have stopped to help, even if it meant taking a chance on touching a dead body. Furthermore, if the man had indeed been dead, they should have stopped to bury him. But because the priest and Levite were probably Sadducees and Sadducees did not honor the oral law, they felt justified in not stopping to help the man because of the demands of the written law.

Obviously, these two religious leaders were more concerned with preserving ritual purity than preserving a life, or at the very least, honoring the man by burying him. In addition, the road to Jericho was so dangerous and robberies so commonplace they had probably grown callous to the sight of another dead, or half-dead, body lying along the wayside. Because many of Jesus's followers and listeners held to the Pharisees' line of religious thought, they would have been indignant—but not surprised—by the priest's and Levite's inaction.

Finally, however, a Samaritan came along—a man despised by the Jews because he was a member of what they considered a mongrel race and a polluted religion, someone with whom the Jews would not so much as consider having a conversation. But this was the man who stopped and, moved by compassion, ministered to the injured man's needs. He didn't just flag down a passing sheepherder or camel driver to call 911, but rather personally tended to his wounds, took him to an inn, cared for him overnight, and then left money for his continued care, promising the innkeeper to return and repay any added cost for the man's needs.

This Samaritan did not limit himself to mumbling a quick prayer for the man's healing, or even to carrying him to the nearest town and dropping him off for someone else to attend to. He gave of himself—his time, his money, his personal attention—even though he knew, in all probability, this man would not have spoken to him had they met under different circumstances. In fact, this Samaritan had no guarantee that, should the man recover and they meet again someday, this Jew would stoop to converse with him even then. And the

> *Jesus makes clear that helping a neighbor, saving a life, is more important than any religious ritual or tradition.*

amazing thing is that, for the most part, Samaritans, like Sadducees, honored the written but not the oral law. This Samaritan, because of his religious beliefs, was bound to ritual purity over the sanctity of human life. Yet the Samaritan, as we see of Jesus so often in the Gospels, was moved by compassion and sacrificed himself in order to minister to this wounded traveler. What a surprise this must have been to Jesus's listeners! The despised Samaritan cast as an unexpected and unlikely hero. Jesus makes clear that helping a neighbor, saving a life, is more important than any religious ritual or tradition.

Rockin' the Boat

No wonder this story has come to be known as the parable of the good Samaritan. This man gave unselfishly, with no thought to personal inconvenience or cost and no anticipation of repayment of any kind. He was quite obviously more concerned with the sanctity of human life than his own schedules or comfort. The good Samaritan was indeed the type of person we all would like to have as a neighbor, for he was a man who heeded a higher calling than self-service and who actively modeled a you-first life to a me-first world.

Even the Jewish law expert could not deny that fact. He acknowledged that the Samaritan, the one who "showed mercy," was the true neighbor. What a shock it must have been to him when Jesus then said, "Go and *do* likewise." The implication is that, should this respected Jewish lawyer come across a despised Samaritan in need, he must put away his preconceived ideas of social and religious status, as well as any concerns about his own convenience, and give himself to care for the Samaritan, regardless of the cost. To refuse to do so would be to break one of the two greatest commandments in the Law: "Love your neighbor as yourself." As He so often did, Jesus had rocked the boat of another member of the religious establishment.

But what of our own boats? Does Jesus's command to "go and do likewise," even among those who have no respect for us or our faith, who may even be openly hostile toward us, rock a few of our boats as well?

Even before coming to the Lord I felt strongly that racism and social and economic inequity were wrong. And yet, I felt powerless to change them. Then, once I became a Christian, I switched my focus to eternal salvation, leaving the righting of those social and economic wrongs to those whose vision did not extend beyond this world. After all, the eternal is much more important than the temporal, right? And didn't Jesus say that the poor would always be with us (see Matthew 26:11)?

> *Yes! We are our brother's keeper, as well as our neighbor's keeper— and that includes everyone, no exceptions.*

Yes, He did. But He also said, "If you want to be perfect, go, sell what you have and give to the poor, and you will have treasure in heaven; and come, follow Me" (Matthew 19:21). Just as He did in the parable of the good Samaritan, Jesus was responding to the haunting question posed by Cain in Genesis 4:9, following the world's first murder: "Am I my brother's keeper?"

Our Lord's answer to that age-old question is a resounding "Yes!" We *are* our brother's keeper, as well as our neighbor's keeper—and that includes everyone, no exceptions. And that makes for a mighty big tidal wave to rock our boats, doesn't it? Because that means we have to open our hearts and our hands, even to those who may despise us—the gay activist, the abortionist, the career criminal— and give of ourselves, *regardless of the cost.* It means it's not enough to protest *against* abortion; we need to work *for* the preservation of life, whether that includes giving of our finances and time to support the local crisis pregnancy center or taking a pregnant woman into our home and possibly even helping to raise her child. It means it's not enough to condemn the sin of homosexuality in an effort to preserve the sanctity of marriage; we must exhibit unconditional love (not approval) to those trapped in that destructive lifestyle, even if they insult us and refuse our love. It means it's not enough to decry the futility of a welfare state and the demeaning cycle it perpetuates; we have to actively seek alternative means to help meet the needs of the economically and socially disadvantaged while at the same time offering them a brighter future with dignity and hope.

> *We have spent a lot of time cursing the darkness, but precious little time lighting candles to dispel that darkness.*

And we have to do all these things whether people respond to our message of the gospel or not.

Uh oh. I think a few boats just capsized. And most of the rest of them are rowing away as fast as they can, leaving a clear message in their wake: "She's preaching a social gospel!"

No, I am not. People need a right relationship with God most of all. But the church is called to offer love in word and deed, helping people with their needs for today and eternity. What I am saying is this: the church has often failed miserably in its responsibility to its neighbors. We have spent a lot of time cursing the darkness, but precious little time lighting candles to dispel that darkness.

Of course, I know there are numerous examples of churches and ministries, large and small, and individual Christians who are doing much for Christ's kingdom by serving their neighbors in America and around the world. Who can forget the tiny, bent figure of Mother Teresa, selflessly pouring out her life to the poorest of the poor in India? Or Corrie ten Boom and her entire family, whose courageous efforts cost some of them their lives but also saved many of the Jewish people from the horrors of the Nazi concentration camps?

And then there are my own personal heroes, Pastor Thank-God and Glory Obi, pastors of the Jesus Victorious Church in Nigeria. These dear ones, who first contacted me through one of my publishers and with whom I have now corresponded for years, eke out a meager existence in a section of their country that is hostile to the Christian faith. Not only are Bibles and Christian literature in short supply, but so are the basic necessities of life, such as food and clothing. Yet every letter I receive from them is filled with praise and thanksgiving to a faithful God, as well as promises to continue praying for my unsaved loved ones here in this land of plenty. Just recently they wrote that they have felt called by God to "take in the truly poor among us"—the prostitutes, the lame, the outcasts—to teach them a trade and offer them an alternative to life on the streets. What precious little they have is now being shared with those who have even less. And yet, what riches these dear people must have awaiting them in heaven!

Countless other believers throughout the world are not only harassed but also actively persecuted, including lengthy prison terms and martyrdom, for their faith in Jesus Christ. How I admire, love, and pray for these dear brothers and sisters who are faithfully serving on the front lines of battle!

So how do we measure up to these committed and faithful warriors? Let's be honest here. For the most part, aren't we satisfied to drop a little extra in the offering plate on "missions Sunday," trusting the church leaders to disperse it equitably? Don't the majority of us drive right by those scruffy individuals standing on street corners with their handwritten signs, "Will work for food," justifying our inaction with the rationalization that it's probably just a scam?

It may be. But aren't they still our neighbors? Don't we still have a responsibility to them beyond "Depart in peace, be warmed and filled" (James 2:16)? Are we truly concerned that if we stop we might be encouraging their sin—in which case we may be justified in continuing on our way—or do we have a greater fear of the time and effort it might take to get involved?

Maybe we did stop once and, after buying lunch for a bedraggled stranger, found ourselves rebuffed in our efforts to talk about Jesus. Or maybe we handed a few dollars for a meal to an old man with sunken eyes and a threadbare jacket, only to see him huddled in a corner a few hours later, drinking from a bottle stuffed inside a brown paper sack. Or maybe, just maybe, we saw so much need around us that we threw up our hands in despair and gave up on trying to help anyone.

> *Jesus confronted people at the point of their sin, but always in love and always with the purpose of seeing them restored to relationship with God.*

Are any of these the responses we would expect from Jesus? Absolutely not. These are responses birthed out of hard hearts, responses that should sound a warning bell in our minds to "guard our heart" against that hardening process that will ultimately cut us off from the voice of God.

Our Savior, whose heart was always soft and tender, was "moved with compassion" when He saw the crowds, "because they were like sheep not having a shepherd" (Mark 6:34). And so, He fed them. He healed them. He comforted them. He taught them. But never, never did He ignore or reject them—even though many rejected Him. His focus was always on others, never on Himself.

Does that mean God has no standards, no boundaries in ministering to those in need—standards and boundaries that should be adopted by those of us who minister in His name? Of course not. God never blesses or ignores sin. Jesus confronted people at the point of their sin, but always in love and always with the purpose of seeing them restored to relationship with God. Nevertheless, He never overlooked someone's need based on the fact that it might be inconvenient or uncomfortable for Him. After all, it doesn't get much more inconvenient or uncomfortable than crucifixion. But it was all about motive—giving of Himself, putting love for God and others first, laying down His life that others might ultimately be delivered from death.

How faithful are we in applying this basic kingdom law to relationships? Do we willingly and regularly place the needs and desires of others ahead of ourselves? Do we model a you-first life to a me-first world?

So, we come back to the beginning: Where is our focus? Who owns our heart? Do we still lay claim to it ourselves? Or have we truly given it over to the only One who can be trusted to keep and seal it for the courts of heaven? Those whose hearts truly belong to Him will not worry about ungodly criticisms from inside the church. (Wasn't Jesus Himself often criticized by the religious?) Those whose hearts belong to God will minister in confidence, knowing they are walking in the footsteps of the Master, holding His hand, modeling His life, and leading others to His side.

Applying the Golden Rule

So how do we practically apply Jesus's ministry of reconciliation, to which we have *all* been called? Jesus said it this way: "Therefore, whatever you want men to do to you, do also to them, for this is the Law and the Prophets" (Matthew 7:12).

This verse, commonly known as the Golden Rule, epitomizes the kingdom law that is at the heart of all relationships. If this kingdom law were understood and put into practice, it would revolutionize society. The problem is that few have understood this law; even fewer have actually put it into practice.

Of course, we can't expect those without hearts of flesh, who are not subjects of God's kingdom, to live by His rules or laws. But what about those of us who have already been translated from the kingdom of darkness into the kingdom of God's Son (see Colossians 1:13)? How faithful are we in applying this basic kingdom law to relationships? Do we willingly and regularly place the needs and desires of others ahead of ourselves? Do we model a you-first life to a me-first world?

Maybe. But I can't help but think that if we did, hurting people would be more likely to go to a church rather than a bar for help. If we did, unbelievers would think of us as joyful people rather than critical ones. If we did, the world would be more apt to see God as an unconditional lover rather than a judgmental, unmerciful ogre.

Author Philip Yancey, in *What's So Amazing About Grace?*, tells the story of a homeless prostitute in such dire straits that she couldn't even feed her two-year-old daughter. When asked why she didn't go to a church for help she answered, "Why would I ever go there? I was already feeling terrible about myself. They'd just make me feel worse."

Yancey then goes on to write:

> *What struck me about my friend's story is that women much like this prostitute fled toward Jesus, not away from him. The worse a person felt about herself, the more likely she saw Jesus as a refuge. Has the church lost that gift? Evidently the down-and-out, who flocked to Jesus when he lived on earth, no longer feel welcome among his followers. What has happened?*

Yancey's contention is that we have ceased to be amazed by grace, that we take for granted God's incredible and costly gift of grace that purchased our pardon from hell. Thus we fail to extend that grace to those who need it most.

Yancey explains it this way in the book:

The world thirsts for grace in ways it does not even recognize.... Some of us seem so anxious about avoiding hell that we forget to celebrate our journey toward heaven. Others of us, rightly concerned about issues in a modern "culture war," neglect the church's mission as a haven of grace in this world of ungrace.

Now I'm not saying that if we suddenly begin extending grace to everyone we meet that they will all fall on their knees and accept Christ. Some people will always reject our message and actively persecute us for it, regardless of our actions. But, if we acted more like Christ, then it would certainly give them less justification to brand us as hypocrites, and a lot more incentive to consider the truth of the gospel.

Fulfilling the Golden Rule is loving our neighbors as ourselves, always keeping in mind that our neighbors include even those who are considered the least in our society. Fulfilling the Golden Rule is as simple—and as difficult—as responding with kindness to someone who is antagonistic toward us, realizing that kindness rather than hurt is what we would like to receive ourselves. It is treating with dignity the one who has sunk to such depths of depravity that virtually all vestiges of the image of God have faded from his being. It is taking the chance to once again reach out with generosity to the one who bit our hand the last time we offered it in love.

Above all, it is the humble realization that we do not have the capacity to do any of these things in our own strength. We have to put God first. Only He can empower us to live above and beyond our own fallen, sinful, me-first nature. And He has done that through His substitutionary death and resurrection and the subsequent sending of His Spirit to live within us. It is that Spirit—the same Spirit who "raised Jesus from the dead" (Romans 8:11)—who is more than sufficient to enable us to model a selfless, you-first life to a desperate and dying world.

Love Conquers

We must choose day by day, hour by hour, minute by minute to live God's way by God's grace. Unfortunately, most of us are not willing to make that choice, at least not on a continual basis. It is so much easier and more natural to react as we did before we had the Spirit of God living within us. We want to look out for number one, justifying our selfishness by painting it with a my-quality-of-life brush. After all, we can always find those who will commiserate with us and agree that we were absolutely justified in defending ourselves, in standing up for our own rights, in demanding equity in the way we are treated.

> *We must choose day by day, hour by hour, minute by minute to live God's way by God's grace.*

Which, of course, is what Jesus did, right? Wrong. The only One who truly had the right to defend Himself, to stand up for His rights, didn't. When offered the chance to refute false charges brought against Him, Jesus kept silent, according to Matthew 26:63. Later, as He stood before the governor, "being accused by the chief priests and elders, He said nothing" (27:12). Even when Pilate himself asked Jesus, "Do You not hear how many things they testify against You?" Jesus "answered him not one word, so that the governor marveled greatly" (vv. 13,14).

Finally, as He hung, naked and bleeding on the cross, Jesus responded to the greatest outpouring of hatred and injustice in the history of mankind by crying out, "Father, forgive them, for they do not know what they do" (Luke 23:34).

God so loved the world He gave His only Son. When Jesus was lifted up on the cross to die, He lifted our load, carrying on His shoulders the very burden of our sins. He paid the required price and bought the necessary pardon, but not without great personal sacrifice. So how is it that we think we can possibly draw anyone to Him if we are not willing to live a life of personal sacrifice, even as He did? How can we justify preaching a God-first, you-first gospel while practicing a me-first lifestyle?

We can't. If our words and our lives don't line up, we are no different than the hypocritical religious leaders of Jesus's day who were spiritually abusing the very people to whom they were supposed to be ministering. For although these religious leaders had good intentions in trying to protect God's Word and keep the people from breaking His laws and commands, their efforts had instead deteriorated into a form of legalistic religion, a perversion of God's intentions.

So just how different are we from them? Have we used the letter of the law to condemn people ("Homosexuality is an abomination to God; therefore, I will not disgrace God's name by befriending someone who practices that lifestyle"; "Abortion is murder; therefore, I have a right to denounce and denigrate those who provide those services"), rather than appropriating the spirit of the law and reaching out to them?

In Romans 12, Paul exhorts us to present our bodies as living sacrifices, serving God with the gifts He has given us and loving others without hypocrisy. He concludes with instructions on how to treat our enemies, overcoming evil with good:

Repay no one evil for evil. Have regard for good things in the sight of all men. If it is possible, as much as depends on you, live peaceably with all men. Beloved, do not avenge yourselves, but rather give place to wrath; for it is written, "Vengeance is Mine, I will repay," says the Lord. Therefore "If your enemy is hungry, feed him; If he is thirsty, give him a drink; For in so doing you will heap coals of fire on his head."
Do not be overcome by evil, but overcome evil with good.
—Romans 12:17–21

Years ago I was working on a writing project about homosexuality and AIDS, and how the church should respond. My focus was a call to unconditional love without condoning sinful behavior. However, that call didn't become real for me until I began to work with a young man named Mark, a homosexual activist with AIDS.

Though he agreed to work with me on the project so I could more clearly understand and explain his position, he also told me from the outset that he hated people like me (Christians) and blamed us for all his problems. He also made me promise I wouldn't "preach at him" during the time we worked together on the project.

I honored my promise, and though it was a rocky relationship, we grew close during the months we worked together. I never preached at him, but he read every chapter, every page, every word of the manuscript, including the Scriptures interspersed throughout. One day, only a couple of weeks after the project was completed, Mark called me and said, "Kathi, do you really believe all that Jesus stuff you wrote about in the book?" I assured him I did, and then he said, "OK, you've got five minutes to tell me why I shouldn't kill myself right now."

> *"OK, you've got five minutes to tell me why I shouldn't kill myself right now."*

It took much longer than five minutes, but by the time we concluded our conversation, Mark had prayed to receive Jesus as His Savior. Two weeks later, he died, but not before calling me one last time, just two days before his death. "Kathi," he said, struggling to breathe, "I'm so tired. I can't wait to go home and see Jesus."

For months I had bit my tongue, forcing myself to remain silent when I wanted so much to preach the gospel to that young man. It wasn't easy, but God's Spirit was speaking to Mark's heart, even when I couldn't. And He was speaking to my heart as well. Where once I would have focused on Mark's behavior and his need for repentance, I learned to focus on loving him instead, on putting his feelings above my own, even when he made snide and sarcastic remarks about my faith. In the end, I realized I had been privileged to partner with God in the ministry of reconciliation, and I now rejoice to know that I will one day see that precious young man again.

Before concluding this chapter, let me clarify one point. Living a you-first life does not mean that we refuse to actively stand for righteousness, or that we accept sin and neglect to lovingly point people in the right direction. We cannot ignore the evil around us. However, we must remember Paul's words to the Ephesians: we don't wrestle with flesh and blood; rather our battle is against unseen forces of wickedness (see 6:12). No matter how rude, obnoxious, or hateful those who want to be our enemies may seem, we must treat them with love. They may be blinded, deceived individuals, but their souls are precious to our Lord, as I learned so clearly in my relationship with Mark. And so, we fight for them, not against them, and we do it on our knees, because "the weapons of our warfare are not carnal but mighty in God for pulling down strongholds" (2 Corinthians 10:4).

By overcoming evil with good and by fighting for others in prayer rather than against them in the flesh, we model a you-first life in a me-first world.

By overcoming evil with good and by fighting *for* others in prayer rather than *against* them in the flesh, we model a you-first life in a me-first world. We will be doing unto others what we would have them do to us. And people will recognize there's something different about us, something in absolute contrast to the dying, me-first world around them. Sadly, many will choose to remain in that dying world. But others will respond by choosing life, joining us in the privileged ministry of reconciliation to which our Lord has called us—regardless of the cost.

Making It Personal

1. Consider your own involvement in different areas of ministry. How do you see those ministries related to the ministry of reconciliation? _____

_____
_____
_____

2. Can you think of someone in your life—past or present— whom you consider ungodly? What would you do if you came across that person, wounded and in deep need of help? _____

_____
_____
_____

3. What evil situations are you up against in your own life? Can you think of any practical ways that you might "overcome evil with good"? _____

_____
_____
_____

4. Read Matthew 7:12. How can you model this kingdom law day-by-day? List some specific things you can do for people in your own life. _____

_____
_____
_____

4

Heart Condition

Search me, O God, and know my heart; Try me, and know
my anxieties; And see if there is any wicked way in me,
And lead me in the way everlasting.
—Psalm 139:23–24

Many of us have seen the bumper sticker that reads: "Christians aren't perfect, just forgiven." Technically, that's a true statement. And it's a handy disclaimer to have on the back of your car if you're one of those Christians who ignores speed limits.

But it can also become a major cop-out when we get nailed for some bad behavior we would rather not change. I much prefer the statement that says: "God loves you just the way you are, but He loves you too much to leave you that way."

Paul in Romans 5:8 declares that God demonstrated, or showed, His love for us "in that while we were still sinners, Christ died for us." And aren't we glad? If Jesus had waited until we were no longer sinners to die for us, it never would have happened. Because we are all part of a fallen race, descended from Adam and Eve, we are sinners by inheritance, by nature. But I also believe there is a point in each of our lives—some theologians refer to it as the "age of accountability"—when we make a conscious decision to commit what we instinctively know to be an act of sin or rebellion. Then we become sinners by action or commission.

From the beginning of time, man has tried to deal with his own sins in his own way. Adam and Eve tried to cover their newly discovered nakedness with fig leaves. (I've got a fig tree in my yard, and when I look at the size of those leaves, I have to believe that either their fig leaves were a lot bigger than the ones on my tree, or they sure used a lot of them!) When they realized the fig leaves—whatever their size—were not going to do the job, they attempted to hide from God. That didn't work either. God found them and replaced their faulty covering of leaves with the skin of an animal, demonstrating the necessity of shedding blood for the forgiveness or remission of sins (see Hebrews 9:22).

Unfortunately, this lesson wasn't fully understood, or applied, by their oldest son, Cain. Genesis tells the story of the first two human offspring, Cain and Abel:

> *And in the process of time it came to pass that Cain brought an offering of the fruit of the ground to the LORD. Abel also brought of the firstborn of his flock and of their fat. And the LORD respected Abel and his offering, but He did not respect Cain and his offering. And Cain was very angry, and his countenance fell.*
> —Genesis 4:3–5

When I first read this story many years ago, it seemed terribly unfair to me. Cain and Abel had each brought to God an offering representing their livelihood. Why did God accept Abel's offering but not Cain's? Did God approve of shepherds but not farmers? To be honest, I couldn't blame Cain for being angry, although I couldn't understand or condone the murder of his brother.

But as I more fully understood the seriousness of sin and the necessity of the shedding of blood for the remission of sins, the story of Cain and Abel began to make sense. Since God had already set the precedent in the Garden of Eden—atoning for sin requires a blood offering—Abel's offering met God's requirement, while Cain's did not. This story is not about two young men bringing to

God an offering of the fruits of their individual labors; it is about whether they would adhere to God's standards of acceptance or foolishly and rebelliously demand to be accepted on their own terms.

The rest, as they say, is history. But the conflict continues to this day. Will we come to God in the way He demands, or will we try to do our own thing? There are countless religions throughout the world, each with its own requirements for reaching God. But only those individuals who approach God on His terms—through the blood of His only Son, Jesus Christ—will be accepted in His sight.

What does all this have to do with guarding our hearts, fulfilling the Great Commandment to love God with all our heart, soul, mind, and strength, and loving our neighbors as ourselves? Everything. For without an understanding of the seriousness of sin and our propensity toward it, as well as the only way God will forgive our sins, we cannot effectively guard our heart against the hardness that prevents the flow of God's life from our heart to others.

The Wages of Sin

When I was ten years old, my German grandfather "Opa" died. My two brothers and I were not allowed to go to the funeral, ostensibly because we were too young to understand death. Although I was upset by my parents' decision at the time, I now know they were right, at least as far as our not understanding death. The problem was, they didn't understand it either. How could they? None of us knew God. None of us had received God's free gift of eternal life, and we were, therefore, subject to the "wages of sin," which is death (see Romans 6:23). And death, for those who have not received eternal life, is a fearful thing to contemplate (see Hebrews 2:14–15).

Despite what some in our culture say, death is more than the cessation of breath or brain waves or heartbeat. Without Christ, it is eternal separation from the One who is the very source of Life itself. It is being eternally cut off from all light, joy, peace, love, truth, and goodness. It is spending eternity with all that represents evil, pain, sorrow, suffering, fear, darkness, and hopelessness. And it lasts forever.

But I didn't know any of that when I was ten years old. All I knew was that I would never again see my Opa. Never again would I feel the bristly kiss of his mustached face against my cheek. Never again would he whittle a wooden toy for my brothers or me. Never again would we sit with him under the grape arbor in his backyard while we waited for our grandmother, Omi, to bring out her freshly baked, melt-in-your-mouth butter cookies.

And it made me very, very sad. But, after crying myself to sleep for a few nights, I got caught up in schoolwork and friends and piano lessons, and the pain of loss began to fade into the everyday busyness of an active child.

Then, in high school, I lost two friends—one in a car accident, one to cancer. This was different. Old people, even beloved grandparents, had, after all, lived on earth for quite a few years. We expect them to die. But teenagers? Girls my own age? Girls whose dreams of marriage and family and careers would never be realized? This was a lot harder to deal with, especially since these deaths occurred soon after my experiences at the convent. If there was nothing I could do to make myself worthy to come into God's presence, had my Opa or my friends fared any better? Or were they burning in an everlasting hell, doomed to spend eternity in agony and torment?

> *No amount of fun and excitement squeezed out of life here on earth could ever make up for the terrors and eternity of hell.*

The hopelessness of it was overwhelming. No amount of fun and excitement squeezed out of life here on earth could ever make up for the terrors and eternity of hell. I had already come to the conclusion that God was holy, and I knew without question that I was not. And even with the minimal Bible training I had received, I knew the truth, if not the exact words, of Hebrews 9:27: "It is appointed for men to die once, but after this the judgment." What I didn't know at that time was the verse immediately following:

"So Christ was offered once to bear the sins of many" (v. 28).

After I became a Christian, I rejoiced in the glorious truth that the wages of my sin had been paid in full when Jesus died in my place. As time went on, however, I began to lose sight of just how costly those wages were. As a result, I started to presume upon God's grace, flippantly asking for forgiveness when I fell, and then going merrily on my way. I had much to learn about confession and cleansing—and the wages of sin.

Getting What We Deserve?

Some years ago I served on a church staff as a biblical counselor. Being the only woman serving on this team of seven counselors, I tended to get the lion's share of counseling appointments, simply because the majority of those who called for counseling were women.

Occasionally, however, I would counsel a husband and wife together, particularly for the first appointment, until I could decide whether they needed to be seen separately or as a couple. In one particular instance, a couple I will call Sam and Michelle came to see me, having scheduled an appointment for marriage counseling. Almost from the outset, Sam made it obvious that he had not come for counseling at all. He was simply there to placate his wife and had no intention of listening to any advice or suggestions from me or anyone else. He certainly wasn't about to listen to anything that he perceived as criticism of him or his behavior.

As I sat across the desk from this couple, listening to Sam list his wife's faults and failures in an effort to justify his constant criticism of her—"She's lazy"; "She doesn't understand me"; "She has never tried to make me happy"—I saw the resignation in Michelle's slumped shoulders and her downcast eyes. I watched an occasional tear escape and roll down her cheek, as I prayed silently: *What, God? What do I say to this man? How do I make him see what his self-centered tirades are doing to his poor wife? Give me a Scripture, Lord, or a word or—*

And suddenly I knew what was at the root of this man's selfish, critical attitude. As soon as he took a breath, I interrupted with a very direct question: "You think you've been cheated, don't you, Sam?"

He jumped as if I'd slapped him. His eyes grew wide. "How did you know?" he asked. "I mean, how—"

I continued. "You think you've missed out, that you deserve something better."

Sam nodded. "Yes," he answered, his voice rising slowly. "That's exactly what I think. I've worked hard all these years, and I'm not getting any younger. I just want...I just want what's coming to me, that's all!"

I took a deep breath, as God spoke powerfully into my heart. "Sam," I said, "what you're telling me is that you want what you deserve. Is that right?"

Sam nodded again. "I sure do," he agreed. "That's all I'm asking for—just what I deserve!"

"Maybe you've forgotten what that is," I said, reaching for the Bible on my desk and opening it to Romans. Sam's eyebrows knitted together in a scowl, but he said nothing as I began to read: "Romans 6:23 tells us: 'The wages of sin is death, but the gift of God is eternal life in Christ Jesus our Lord.' Are you familiar with that Scripture, Sam?"

"Of course I am," he answered. "I got saved when I was 17. I've been in church most of my life, and I read my Bible every day. So what's that verse got to do with me?"

> *"Sam, if Jesus hadn't paid the wages of sin for us, we wouldn't have eternal life. We'd have what we all deserve— death and hell."*

"Perhaps," I said, lowering my voice a notch, "it's God's way of reminding us of what it is we really deserve." I let that sink in for a moment, and then went on. "Sam, if Jesus hadn't paid the wages of sin for us, we wouldn't have eternal life. We'd have what we all deserve, death and hell."

Michelle's head snapped up and her eyes opened wide, as her husband exploded out of his chair. "Are you trying to tell me that

God is going to send me to hell just because I want something better than what I've got?" Sam's eyes blazed as he glared down at me. "Because if you are," he went on, "I don't believe you. This isn't the Old Testament days, you know. We live under grace, so God will forgive me, even if I don't treat my wife like I should."

Sam appeared to be as shocked as Michelle when he realized what he had said. For several moments, the words seemed to hang in the air. I wanted to say so many things, but I knew the Lord had placed His hand over my mouth.

Then Sam crumpled. As he fell back into his chair, the tears came and his shoulders shook with sobs. Michelle forgot her own pain and reached out to her husband, enveloping him in an embrace of unconditional love. Sam was under too much conviction to resist. As they cried together, I left them alone for a few moments, then returned to start the long process of healing and restoration.

Sadly, not all such counseling encounters turn out so positively. But for those willing to own the fact that we are all sinners who deserve death and hell, and that we should, therefore, praise and thank God from a grateful heart, there is always hope for healing and restoration. And that, of course, is the ultimate purpose of any counseling session.

For me, the time with Sam and Michelle was a period of intense self-examination and recommitment in my own life. The reason my confrontation with Sam affected me so deeply was that I too needed a fresh revelation about repentance and grace. As I meditated on what it was that I truly deserved, I was shaken to the core of my being. How lightly I had taken God's promise of forgiveness and cleansing in 1 John 1:9: "If we confess our sins, He is faithful and just to forgive us our sins and to cleanse us from all unrighteousness."

"If we confess our sins..." How long had I oversimplified the word *confess*? How many times had I tossed off a "Sorry, God," assuming that constituted a confession and I was now cleansed and forgiven? As I began to study the word's meaning, I realized how much deeper true confession is than merely saying, "I'm sorry."

In the Greek, the word *confess* comes from two other words, which, when combined, mean to come into agreement with what God says about something. In the case of 1 John 1:9 that would mean we need to come into agreement with what God says about sin. And what is that? "The wages of sin is death" (Romans 6:23).

So if I truly want to be forgiven for my sin and cleansed of all unrighteousness, I need to do more than simply say, "I'm sorry about what I did, God." I need to agree with God that the sin I committed—whether it is something as outrageous as robbing a bank or shooting my neighbor, or as seemingly trivial as saying an unkind word about someone or having a bad attitude—is deserving of death. I also need to realize that if Jesus had not died for that very sin, no matter how outrageous or trivial it may seem to me, I would spend eternity in hell because of it.

Sort of puts a whole different light on getting what we deserve, doesn't it? It surely did for me, and, thankfully, for Sam.

Our Greatest Enemy

We hear a lot in the church today about spiritual warfare—and that's good. We need to know how to stand and fight against the devil and his demonic hordes that are bent on our destruction (see John 10:10; Ephesians 6:12). But the key to victory over Satan is found in James 4:7: "Therefore, *submit to God*. Resist the devil and he will flee from you" (emphasis added).

I have heard that Scripture misquoted more often than not. Many people love the last part of that verse and can quote it quite handily: "Resist the devil and he will flee from you." But the problem comes when we try to "do" the second part of the verse without heeding the first part: "Therefore, submit to God."

> *Every battle we fight is won or lost at the point of deciding whether we will submit our will to God's.*

There's that word again: *therefore.* What is it referring to here? It's referring to the previous six verses, which speak to the problems that arise from pride and the subsequent need to walk in humility.

Therefore, we need to submit ourselves to God, because in ourselves we can't walk in humility. And as long as pride has any place in our lives, the enemy has a hook in us and will use it to pull us away from God.

When we try to resist the devil in our own strength, he does not flee from us, he laughs at us! He knows we are no match for him. But when we humbly acknowledge our inability to resist him on our own, submitting ourselves to God and allowing Him to show us the "way of escape" (1 Corinthians 10:13), the devil knows he has lost the battle, and he moves on—at least for a while.

Our greatest enemy, therefore, is not the devil—God takes care of him. Our greatest enemy is a hard heart. Every battle we fight is won or lost at the point of deciding whether we will submit our will to God's, whether we will take God's way of escape or try to manufacture our own. And that decision will reflect either the hardened or softened condition of our heart, which, again, is why the Scripture admonishes us "above all" to guard our hearts.

A soft, tender heart will always yield to God more quickly than one that has areas of hardness in it. Though we as Christians have been given new hearts—a "heart of flesh" to replace the "stony heart" (Ezekiel 11:19)—we must daily ask God to search us and to point out any hard, unyielding, sinful places. We then confess and allow His Spirit to deal with those places. If we continue to resist Him, we will have difficulty discerning God's direction and call for our daily lives. In our wandering, we will miss out on His best for us.

Learning to Follow God's Lead

Like Adam and Eve in the Garden of Eden, God has provided a covering for our sins. Their covering, of course, was temporary, pointing toward the permanent covering to come, which we have now received, Jesus Christ. The question is: If our sins are permanently covered because of the once-for-all redemptive work at Calvary, why do we still struggle with what seems to be the old nature, which draws us toward sin and evil?

Even though we have already been redeemed and our salvation is secure, the redemption and rebuilding of our soul is still in progress. We will not be completely formed into Christ's image until we see Him face-to-face. We struggle. We are tempted. We fall. We are in a moment-by-moment battle (see 1 Peter 2:11).

Emotions are a wonderful thing. God gave them to us so we could relate to Him and to others. After all, loving God with all our heart, mind, soul, and strength, and loving our neighbor as ourselves involves more than a mental assent to do so. But emotions, when not submitted to God, can get us into a lot of trouble. When we allow our emotions to call the shots, we are like the man described in James 1:6,8: "a wave of the sea driven and tossed by the winds...unstable in all his ways." Living by emotions is like living on a never-ending roller coaster of highs and lows—perpetual immaturity.

The devil also wreaks havoc with our thought life when we fail to allow God to transform us by the renewing of our minds (see Romans 12:2). When we were unsaved, we did not take account of God in our thought processes. We based our decisions and opinions on tangible things—what we could perceive with our senses or reason with our mind. But after being born again by the Holy Spirit, we have access to the very heart and mind of God, primarily through reading His Word and meditating on Scripture. We also have the ability to grow and become more like Him, and then to teach and train others to do the same.

But we have to avail ourselves of this privilege by seeking God in prayer, by reading and applying the Bible to our daily lives, by consciously rejecting worldly thoughts and viewpoints that conflict with God's Word (see 2 Corinthians 10:5), and by keeping our hearts tender and sensitive toward God's direction and guidance. And that, according to Hebrews 5:12–14, takes practice:

For though by this time you ought to be teachers, you need someone to teach you again the first principles of *the oracles of God; and you have come to need milk and not solid food. For everyone who partakes only of milk is unskilled in the word of righteousness, for he is a babe. But solid food belongs to **those who are of full age**, that is, those who **by reason of use have their senses exercised to discern both good and evil** (emphasis added).*

The writer of Hebrews is saying that those who are not skilled in reading, understanding, and applying the Word of God to their lives are spiritual babies, unable to recognize the difference between the world's way of thinking and doing things and God's way. It doesn't matter how long they may have been saved. But those who are mature have come to be so by "exercising" their senses to discern (or differentiate) between good and evil. How do we exercise our senses to discern between good and evil? By continually, faithfully, and humbly reading, studying, meditating on, and applying God's Word to our lives—and by yielding to God's Spirit when He spotlights something in the Bible that jumps out at us and says, "This is for you. Now. Today. Let Me make this change in you."

When that happens, I believe weare experiencing the dividing of soul and spirit by the Word of God, which "is living and powerful, and sharper than any two-edged sword...a discerner of the thoughts and intents of the heart" (Hebrews 4:12). God's Word is showing us

Will we say "yes" to God and allow Him to change our heart, to keep it soft, and to make us more like Him?

the difference between God's way (good) and our way (evil). So, we are faced with a choice: Will we submit ourselves to God's will, allowing His Word and His Spirit to change our thinking by replacing our old thoughts with His new ones? Will we say "yes" to God and allow Him to change our heart, to keep it soft, and to make us more like Him? Will we exercise our senses to discern between good and evil so we might become mature believers whom God can use to help teach and train others?

Or will we harden our heart, as did the Israelites of old, who experienced God's miraculous intervention and deliverance in their lives yet quickly turned back to their old ways when things got tough? Hebrews 3:7–11 warns against just such a choice:

> *Today, if you will hear His voice, Do not harden your hearts as in the rebellion, In the day of trial in the wilderness, where your fathers tested Me, tried Me, and saw My works forty years. Therefore I was angry with that generation, And said, 'They always go astray in their heart, And they have not known My ways.' So I swore in My wrath, 'They shall not enter My rest.'"*

To choose to harden our hearts and go our own way rather than God's is to choose the way of sin rather than the way of the Spirit. Living by the Spirit, we make our choices and decisions based on the guidance and direction of God's Word. The Spirit gives life; putting our desires above God's will produces death. By resisting God's Word we open the door to the one who is referred to as the "enemy of our soul," the devil himself. And as we saw earlier, when we try to resist the devil in our own strength, it doesn't work. Rather than fleeing from us, he laughs at us, as he plants his deceptive thoughts in our mind, toys with our emotions, and weakens our will.

> *The Spirit gives life; putting our desires above God's will produces death.*

A Christian stubbornly resisting the Spirit's leading is vulnerable to the devil's attacks and cannot fulfill the greatest commandments of all, the commandments that encompass "all the Law and the Prophets": to love God with all our heart, soul, mind, and strength, and to love our neighbor as ourselves. Such a Christian is in rebellion, and apart from repentance, her heart will continue to grow harder and harder until the voice of God grows too faint to be discerned amidst the deafening noise of countless other voices vying for our attention.

Failing to Hear

Having served in prison ministry for several years, I saw the sad reality of this truth many times. I considered it a great privilege to lead groups of inmates in Bible study, as well as ministering to them one-on-one. What amazed me most was how many of the prisoners had been raised in Christian homes and had even made commitments to Christ at some point in their life. Nonetheless, because they failed to read and obey God's Word, instead hardening their hearts and misappropriating God's grace and forgiveness, they became

> *What amazed me most was how many of the prisoners had been raised in Christian homes and had even made commitments to Christ at some point in their life.*

entrenched in sin. Almost without exception, as I spoke with inmates who had a Christian background, they admitted that they no longer thought about the depth of their own sinfulness and how great a price had been paid to redeem them from the wages of that sin. Relearning this great truth became the starting point for their restoration.

If we are not submitting to the rule of Christ in our lives, another problem may surface. It may not manifest itself in outright rebellion or sin that lands us in such dire straits as prison. However, it is serious. A stubborn heart may render us unable to discern God's will for our lives, and we may miss out on wonderful opportunities for our growth.

For instance, before I started the project during which I worked with Mark, the homosexual activist who later received Christ, I was happily working on a couple of other less stressful and less controversial topics—and I liked it that way. When the possibility of the new assignment came my way, I wanted nothing to do with it. However, when pressed, I agreed to pray about it.

I did, of course, but not with an open heart. My prayer was more along the lines of: "God, You know how busy I am already and all the things I'm already working on, so I know it couldn't be Your will for me to take on something new. And especially not this! I don't even know anything about homosexuality or AIDS, and to be perfectly honest, I don't want to. Please bring someone else to take this assignment, God, and if You want to use me to help find that person, I'm willing." Certainly not a humble prayer of surrender!

I had my own agenda, and it did not include working on this new project. I continued to pray for God to bring along someone else or to show me if I was supposed to find that person, but I heard nothing in response. Nothing.

Finally, however, I became so disturbed by God's perceived lack of response that I said: "OK, Lord, whatever You want from me, I'll do. I'm listening, and I'm ready to obey." That's when the answer came, and I knew I was supposed to accept the assignment. Almost immediately, after submitting to God's will and purpose in this situation, I met Mark...and the rest is history.

God seldom answers my prayers for direction when I've already come up with an agenda of my own. Why? Because, at the time, I care more about what I want than what God wants. I'm trusting myself, rather than Him; I'm looking to my wisdom, rather than to His. I have already made a me-first choice: to go my way instead of God's way.

And so, once again, we come back to God's way of escape, which is to stay in His Word, loving Him with all our heart, mind, soul, and strength. There simply is no other answer. Are we standing on the right foundation? Are we trusting Him and submitting ourselves to His will, or are we on a faulty foundation, still making choices in our own strength and human wisdom? If we truly love Him, we will trust Him and gladly submit to Him and to His ways. But when we find ourselves making the choice to go our own way, our love for Him is not complete. There are still hard spots in our heart.

> *If we truly love Him, we will trust Him and gladly submit to Him and to His ways.*

How do we get rid of them? Like David, we should pray: "Search me, O God, and know my heart; Try me, and know my anxieties; And see if there is any wicked way in me, And lead me in the way everlasting" (Psalm 139:23–24).

If this is our sincere desire, we can be confident that God will be faithful to answer. When He shows us those wicked ways— those hard spots in our hearts—and we, in turn, submit them to Him, He will melt them away with His great love. He truly does love us just the way we are, but, thankfully, He loves us too much to leave us that way.

Making It Personal

1. Can you remember a time when you became aware that you had done something wrong—that you had sinned, whether or not you used that term—and tried to deal with it yourself? What did you do, and what was the outcome? _____

_____

_____

_____

_____

_____

_____

2. Keeping in mind that, apart from Jesus and His sacrificial gift for us, we deserve nothing but death and eternal separation from God, make a list of the many blessings God has bestowed upon you simply because He loves you. Then thank God just for who He is.

_____

_____

_____

_____

_____

_____

_____

_____

_____

3. Describe a time when you felt you were unable to discern God's will in a particular situation, only to discover that you really weren't open to His answer._____

_____

_____

_____

_____

_____

_____

_____

_____

_____

_____

4. Read Psalm 139:23–24 as a personal prayer. Then write down those things that God's Spirit brings to your mind, asking Him to forgive you and to give you a willing heart to go His way instead of yours._____

_____

_____

_____

_____

_____

_____

_____

_____

_____

_____

_____

5

A Tale of Two Sons—
and the Father's Heart

But the father said to his servants, "Bring out the best robe and put it on him, and put a ring on his hand and sandals on his feet. And bring the fatted calf here and kill it, and let us eat and be merry; for this my son was dead and is alive again; he was lost and is found."
—Luke 15:22–24

Most of us are familiar with the parable of the prodigal son, but here's a brief synopsis: A well-to-do Jewish farmer had two sons. The younger son wasn't willing to wait for his inheritance until his father died, so he took his portion and set out on his own, traveling far from home and squandering his money until he was reduced to poverty. To support himself, he was forced to take a job feeding pigs, the lowliest position imaginable for someone of Jewish heritage.

The miserable young man soon found himself so hungry that he actually considered eating the slop he was feeding the pigs. That's when he finally came to his senses and realized that even his father's servants were living better than he was. So he set off for home, rehearsing his speech of repentance and hoping his father would have pity on him and allow him to return as a hired hand.

As he trudged home, stoop-shouldered and dejected, the father, who had been watching and waiting for his son's return, spotted him in the distance and ran to meet him, throwing his arms around him and welcoming him home with such obvious joy that the son was astounded. Before the young man could complete his speech of repentance, the father had ordered a royal robe to be put on his shoulders, sandals on his feet, and a ring on his finger. The once rebellious and foolish prodigal, who only recently had been feeding pigs, now found himself the guest of honor at an extravagant party.

The older son, however, who had remained at home working in his father's fields while the younger son was off squandering his inheritance, heard the commotion of the welcoming party and asked one of the servants what was going on. When he found out that his father was throwing a party for his younger brother, who had just returned penniless and smelling of the pigsty, he was angry and stayed out in the fields rather than going in to join the celebration. When his father went out to urge him to come inside, the son refused, complaining at his father's injustice in welcoming home such a worthless prodigal. The father then reminded his older son that, unlike the younger son, he had always been with the father, and was heir to all that the father had. Then he added: "It was right that we should make merry and be glad, for your brother was dead and is alive again, and was lost and is found" (Luke 15:32).

"It was right..." I'm so glad the father said those words, because I so relate to the prodigal. Don't we all, at least those of us who are Christians? Each of us, at some point, had to turn away from the pigsty and begin the long walk home from the far country to the Father, wondering if there was any chance for us, hoping He would receive us.

And, of course, like the father in the parable, He did—lovingly, lavishly, unreservedly—welcome us. Before we had traveled far on that lonely road from the pigsty into the presence of God, He was there, scooping us up in His arms and welcoming us with an unconditional love that amazed and transformed us. Not only did

He forgive our wanderings in the far country and our wallowing with the pigs, He covered us with a royal robe of righteousness and threw a party in our honor. We were home where we belonged, and all of heaven rejoiced.

Our reunion with the Father is a moment frozen in time, etched in our memories as the turning point of our lives—more than that, of our birth into a new life, one that would never end. Who could forget such a monumental occurrence?

Not only did He forgive our wanderings in the far country and our wallowing with the pigs, He covered us with a royal robe of righteousness and threw a party in our honor.

And yet, we sometimes do—maybe not the event itself, but the implications of it. As a result, the unconditional love and grace of the Father who forgave us and welcomed us home ceases to amaze us. Hardness sets in, and we forget who we are, as well as the purpose to which we have been called. And that is a tragedy of such magnitude we scarcely can begin to comprehend it.

How can we ensure that we never take for granted the Love that enabled us to escape the pigpen and then welcomed us home from our rebellious journey? Only by never losing sight of the pain that journey caused the One who was left behind, waiting.

Henri J. M. Nouwen, in *The Return of the Prodigal Son*, explains it this way:

> *The immense joy in welcoming back the lost son hides the immense sorrow that has gone before. The finding has the losing in the background, the returning has the leaving under its cloak. Looking at the tender and joy-filled return, I have to dare to taste the sorrowful events that preceded it. Only when I have the courage to explore in depth what it means to leave home, can I come to a true understanding of the return.*

As I meditate on those words, I cannot help but relive my own moment of revelation when I realized that my hardened, wandering heart has the power to crush the very heart of God. It is at the point of understanding the immense depth of the Father's love—and His sorrow when we fail to return that love—that our hearts are sealed to His. But the moment we cease to listen to the beating of His heart, our own hearts drift off on another journey, back to the far country, away from the Father and into the pigsty. For the leaving comes so much easier to us than the returning.

The Leaving

Just how deeply was the father affected by his son's leaving? To understand that, we must understand the culture in which the story was first told. Author and scholar Kenneth E. Bailey writes the following in *Poet and Peasant*:

> *For over fifteen years I have been asking people of all walks of life from Morocco to India and from Turkey to the Sudan about the implications of a son's request for his inheritance while the father is still living. The answer has almost always been emphatically the same.... [T]he conversation runs as follows:*
>
> *"Has anyone ever made such a request in your village?"*
> *"Never!"*
> *"Could anyone ever make such a request?"*
> *"Impossible!"*
> *"If anyone ever did, what would happen?"*
> *"His father would beat him, of course!"*
> *"Why?"*
> *"This request means—he wants his father to die!"*

The younger son's request for his inheritance was more than selfish, inconsiderate, and hurtful—it was tantamount to a death wish for his father. And everyone in the surrounding towns and villages knew it. The depth and callousness of the insult was unheard of, incomprehensible, unimaginable. The son was asking for more than his portion of the inheritance, he was asking for the right to dispose of it however he wished.

If, in an extreme case, a father signed over his possessions to his son, the father still had the right to live off of the proceeds of those goods until he died. In the case of the prodigal, the boy had no intention of holding his inheritance in reserve for his father's well-being; his only concern was to take the money and spend it on himself.

What a hard-hearted rejection of his father, his home, his entire culture! As surely as Esau had done, the prodigal son "despised his birthright" (Genesis 25:34), severing all ties to his past heritage as well as any hope for a future reconciliation.

The father with the broken heart stood vigil, day after day, hoping against hope that his wayward son would one day appear on the horizon.

And so, he left, going off to a "far country," away from everything familiar, where he "wasted his possessions with prodigal [excessive, reckless, extravagant, unrestrained] living" (Luke 15:13; author's amplification in brackets). Meanwhile, the brokenhearted father had to deal not only with the pain of his son's leaving, but with the shock waves caused by that leaving. Throughout the community, everyone knew what had happened. Righteous anger and indignation toward the son and sympathy for the father undoubtedly were the first reactions. But what about when they saw the father, day after day, gazing longingly down the road, watching and hoping for the return of his treacherous son, the one who had wished him dead? What did they think then?

No doubt the old man became the local laughingstock. Any respect he may have had in the community quickly disappeared. Possibly even his servants scoffed at him behind his back.

But no matter. The father with the broken heart stood vigil, day after day, hoping against hope that his wayward son would one day appear on the horizon. And so, he did.

The Returning

The more often I read or meditate on this particular parable, the more amazed I am that it took me so long to see its true focus, which of course is not so much the returning son as it is the waiting, welcoming father. As short as the parable is, the reader knows what went on in the son's life during his absence: He spent his inheritance on extravagant, self-indulgent living until he had nothing left; then he got a job feeding pigs until he realized how foolish he had been and decided to go home.

But what about the father? What went on in his life during his son's absence? Undoubtedly he had to continue with the day-to-day requirements of overseeing what was left of the estate. While one-third of it had been liquidated and given to the younger son, the remaining two-thirds now belonged to the older son, although the father's prerogative was to continue to live on and oversee the farm until his death. The father also had to interact with other people in various settings, transact business, and so forth. Was he able to go on without any hint of the aching void in his heart? Or did his eyes wander, even when someone was speaking to him, to that empty place on the horizon where he had last seen his son, disappearing into the sunset without so much as a backward glance? Did the old man's jaws clench as he tried to block out the whispers and snickers—or worse yet, the pitying stares—of those who knew he still watched and waited for the one who had so totally rejected him? As he stood at the top of the road, straining his eyes to glimpse a lone figure moving toward him, did his own reason and emotions war within him?

Regardless of our children's age or the path they choose to take, our heart goes with them.

Or did he trust with certainty that the day would surely come when his faithfulness would be rewarded and his aching arms would once again wrap around the man-child who so held his heart? He must have. The only other option would have been to harden his heart and write the boy off as lost forever.

For the old man—as for all of us who have ever wept and prayed over a beloved prodigal—the latter was no option at all. It's been said that deciding to have a child is like deciding to let your heart walk around outside your body for the rest of your life. I don't know the origin of that saying, but as a mother I can attest to its truth. Regardless of our children's age or the path they choose to take, our heart goes with them.

The waiting, of course, is the hardest. I remember it well. When I had a wandering prodigal of my own—my youngest son, who wandered for several years in the wilderness of rebellion against his family, his faith, and everything else familiar—I would meet weekly with a dear friend who had not one, but two prodigals. We shed tears together, did our best to encourage each other, and prayed for our children's return.

During one of those times, we wondered how many other mothers and fathers were dealing with similar situations. So we ran a notice in our church bulletin and newsletter and were overwhelmed at the response. Within weeks we had a list of some 50 brokenhearted parents, longing for encouragement and support, looking for prayer partners. And so, we paired up these parents, knowing from our own experience how sharing the burden can make the pain more tolerable.

But the father in our story had no one to help carry his burden, at least not as far as we know. His vigil indeed was a lonely one, and possibly a long one as well. The story doesn't really give us a time frame, but when our children reject us and everything we stand for, choosing to walk a rebellious and dangerous road to a far country, each day of waiting seems an eternity.

And yet, there is one thing that exceeds the depth of pain a parent feels at a child's departure for the far country—the joy of the returning! Those of us who have experienced it can certainly attest to that. And what portrait of that joy could compare to the one given in this parable: "And he arose and came to his father. But when he was still a great way off, his father saw him and had compassion, and ran and fell on his neck and kissed him" *(*Luke 15:20*)*.

"When he was still a great way off..." While the son was still rehearsing what he was going to say to his father, while he was just a speck on the horizon, the father saw him. Can't you just imagine his heart racing as that tiny speck moved toward him? *Could it be? Is it possible?* As the speck drew nearer, the father's straining eyes identified the familiar outline. Even the threadbare clothes, the stooped shoulders, and the hanging head couldn't hide him now. And so, the father, oblivious to protocol and dignity, hiked up his robe (they didn't wear pants in those days!) and ran—not walked or sauntered or marched, but *ran*—toward his returning son.

Again, we have to keep in mind the culture of the day. This man's farm probably was not in some isolated area outside of town where no one could see this reunion. I can imagine the prodigal had to make that long walk home through familiar towns and villages, past the houses and farms of people he had known all his life—people who knew of his folly and rebellion, of his arrogant departure and insult to his father, people who now watched him return in shame and defeat.

Doubtless he endured numerous icy stares and turned backs, and overheard many snide remarks as he wearily trudged home:

"Well, look who's coming back! Hardly the conquering hero, is he?"

"I didn't have to look—I smelled him coming!"

"What do you suppose his father will do when he sees him?"

"I know what I'd do. I'd have my servants throw him off my property! He'd know in no uncertain terms that he's no longer a son of mine!"

But just when the son thought he could bear no more, just as he was about to give up any hope of reconciliation, the voices stopped. A hush fell over the countryside until the only sounds he could hear were his own shuffling footsteps and...

Slowly, he raised his head. His eyes widened at the sight of the familiar figure racing toward him. The son took a deep breath. Would he have a chance to speak before the old man ordered him back to the pigsty?

Before he could open his mouth, he was nearly bowled over by the impact of his father's embrace. Instead of recriminations, he received kisses. Instead of condemnation, tears of joy. Instead of a cold shoulder, a warm welcome.

The prodigal had returned, and it was time to celebrate.

The Older Son

But it wasn't just the neighbors who were shocked by the father's seemingly outrageous behavior in welcoming the prodigal home again. Someone much closer to the entire situation—someone who lived in the same house and was descended from the same bloodline—was also indignant, and quite resentful, over this scandalous reunion.

So much has been said by so many regarding the younger son, and most of us have no problem relating his story to our own. But how much have we understood about the older son, and how closely have we related to his life?

For those of us who have more than one child, we know how different each can be from the other. We also know that, though we love all our children equally, we also love them differently, particularly when it comes to our firstborn. Something about that firstborn child captures our heart in a way we never thought possible. How well I remember gazing in awe at "Little Al," my own firstborn. Named after his father and both grandfathers, he seemed to me the most beautiful and perfect baby who ever lived. I counted his fingers and toes, traced the softness of his skin, marveled at the intricacy of God's handiwork. True, I experienced many of those same emotions when my other two sons, Michael and Chris, were born. But there is always a special place in our hearts for our firstborn, regardless of how many children we have afterward. For that reason, I can't help but believe that the father in our story possessed a deep, encompassing love for his eldest son.

A cursory reading of the verses in Luke 15 pertaining to this older son gives us a picture of a dutiful, if somewhat churlish and petty young man. I have heard it taught that the older son represents the unsaved, those who have never come to relationship with the Father. I suppose that's possible, but I don't think so. The older son lived on his father's estate, and the father called him *son*. Surely he was part of the family, and a dearly beloved part at that.

Furthermore, the father, in speaking to the older son, referred to the prodigal as *your brother*. In response, however, the older son transferred ownership of the prodigal back to the father by calling him *this son of yours*, intimating that the father was somehow at fault for having sired such a damaged progeny.

The older son's attempt to pass blame to the blameless seems reminiscent of Adam in the Garden. "It's her fault," Adam declared, pointing at Eve. "The woman *You* gave me—she made me do it" (see Genesis 3:12). Adam wasn't so much passing the blame to Eve as he was implying that God had given him a faulty mate. The older brother in the parable, though quick to point out the younger brother's faults, similarly worded his criticism to make clear his disapproval of his father's actions in restoring the unworthy son.

The striking difference in these two stories becomes obvious in their conclusions. After the Fall, God declares that Adam and Eve must leave the Garden, the place of joy and intimate fellowship with the Father, to go out to work the earth. In the story of the prodigal, the father begs his older son to leave the fields and come join the family in their joyous celebration. The son, however, refuses, choosing instead to remain just outside the father's home that he might nurse his grudge and justify his ungracious attitude.

No, I do not see the older son as representing those who have never known God. Instead, I believe he represents those of us who have made our way home from the far country, only to forget the price that was paid to enable us to return. The older son had lost touch with the father's heart, causing his own heart to grow hard and indifferent, not only toward the suffering of his younger brother but also toward the suffering of his father. He was so indifferent to his father's suffering that he was willing to compound it by refusing to join in the celebration, even going so far as to indict his father and condemn his actions. The older son's hard heart had become so focused on himself that he had ceased to appreciate the loving-kindness of his father, as well as the abundance that surrounded him by right of his sonship. He had come to take his father's love for granted and had chosen to shut himself away from it, concentrating instead on proper performance rather than right relationship. In his obsession to *do* all the right things, he had forgotten who he was. He was so blinded by his hard heart that he couldn't see that the very sin for which he condemned his

> *Each time my heart begins to lose touch with the Father's heart, I find myself on another journey to the far country.*

brother—selfishness—was the same sin ruling his own life. He had turned his back on his father; he had lost his sense of identity. And people who lose their own identity no longer have the ability to recognize the identity of others. Instead, they are content to judge and condemn.

Sound familiar? Ever been there? I have—many times. Each time my heart begins to lose touch with the Father's heart, I find myself on another journey to the far country. I may not be heading off in conscious rebellion, like the younger son, determined to sever my connection to the Father and do my own thing, but I am leaving nonetheless.

This is the point at which I relate to the older son. He didn't go out and waste his inheritance on prodigal living. Instead he chose to remain in visible, respectable proximity to his father, *maintaining right actions while cultivating wrong attitudes.* The inevitable result is that both the older son and I end up pointing fingers of judgment at others, not realizing the deep-seated sin in our own hearts.

Like the older son, I forget my identity—a pigsty refugee in a royal robe, given not for merit but out of mercy. And it crushes my Father's heart. My hardened, wandering heart brings grief and sorrow to the only One who loves me with an unconditional, unending, unmerited love.

What fools we all can be! We trade love for license, faithfulness for fear, and limitless grace for unrewarding labor. The call of the far country is a compelling siren song, but it is a counterfeit life, an empty promise, and a cheap substitute for the Father's love.

Becoming Like the Father

Whether we relate more to the older son or to the younger, we must realize our calling is to become like the father. God's purpose for us is not that we should forever be rebellious children leaving and returning, or dutiful children who are content to live on the fringes of the Father's kingdom, grumbling about our own self-imposed martyrdom. The Father has invited us inside, into His very presence, where our hardened hearts will be melted and our demeanor changed to reflect the gracious love of God Himself.

And how desperately we need that change! God freely gives of Himself. We, on the other hand, grasp. We thrive on selfishness. We feed it. We nurse it. We pamper it. We indulge ourselves in it at the expense of those around us. By indulging our selfishness, we add to the pain of the One who already suffers beyond our understanding. In *Lament for a Son*, Nicholas Wolterstorff reflects on the Father's pain: "God is not only the God of the sufferers but the God who suffers. The pain and fallenness of humanity have entered into his heart."

Wolterstorff continues:

It is said of God that no one can behold his face and live. I always thought this meant that no one could see his splendor and live. A friend said perhaps it meant that no one could see his sorrow and live. Or perhaps his sorrow is splendor.

In our selfishness, we forget the sorrow of the One who loves us most, the One whose very suffering reflects the tenderness and vulnerability of His magnificent heart. At times it is difficult even to comprehend that this great God, the Creator of the universe, can experience sorrow. And yet, as I have already mentioned, the Scriptures tell us that His heart is crushed by our wanderings. When we fail to see God as One who sorrows, we miss a major dimension of His personality—and we miss the comfort He longs to give us in our own sorrows.

I will never forget the incident that brought this truth into focus for me. I had just met a couple, Bob and Christine, who had moved into our neighborhood. They had recently adopted two Korean orphans, a brother and sister. As Christine told the story of how they had come to finalize the adoption of these two delightful children, she began by telling me of the tragedy that led to their openness to adopt.

Bob and Christine Rich had a son, Bobby, their only child. At the age of 12, he was killed by a drunk driver. In my book *A Moment a Day*, edited with Mary Beckwith, Christine described the depth of her pain in these words:

> *The darkness of death shrouded me as I began the long and treacherous journey through the grief process. I was unprepared and unskilled at sorrow. Every new phase crashed in upon me with feelings of uncertainty and despair. The God I loved and trusted had disappeared and left me forsaken. My faith, which had been the solid base of my life, exploded into millions of tiny pieces. I had no reason to live on.*

One day they went to their pastor to talk through all that had happened. As they poured out their grief, the wise minister listened. When it seemed they had run out of words, he looked at them with great compassion. With tears in his eyes and a catch in his voice, he asked, "Can you hear the Father crying with you?"

> **With tears in his eyes and a catch in his voice, he asked, "Can you hear the Father crying with you?"**

The couple caught a shared vision of their heavenly Father grieving with them in their loss. At the same time they also caught their first glimmer of hope—hope that they just might make it through. And they have made it through. Today, though they still miss Bobby, as they always will, they rejoice in the privilege of raising two new children.

Neither toughness nor a positive outlook nor even the encouragement of friends carried Bob and Christine through their tragedy. It was the truth of God's own sorrow, God's compassion for them, that helped them survive.

Isaiah 53:3 describes Jesus as a "man of sorrows and acquainted with grief." Verse 4 goes on to say, "Surely He has borne our griefs and carried our sorrows." When Jesus saw Mary and Martha's sorrow over the death of their brother, Lazarus, He wept (see John 11:35). As He stood on the Mount of Olives, overlooking Jerusalem, He grieved over the coming destruction (see Matthew 23:37–39; Luke 19:41–44).

Yes, Jesus was well acquainted with sorrow and grief. And yet, didn't He say, "I and My Father are one" (John 10:30)? Didn't He also say, "He who has seen Me has seen the Father" (14:9)? So how can we doubt that God the Father is also acquainted with grief and sorrow? Why should we be surprised to think that He weeps with us? Jesus wept; therefore, our Father weeps too. And because His heart is so much bigger and infinitely more tender than ours, His sorrow must greatly exceed ours as well.

> God's heart is crushed when we depart from Him—whether we depart physically like the prodigal son, or remain on the outskirts of His presence, nursing a hard heart like the older son.

"I was crushed by their adulterous heart which has departed from Me" (Ezekiel 6:9). God's heart is crushed when we depart from Him—whether we depart physically like the prodigal son, or remain on the outskirts of His presence, nursing a hard heart like the older son. But we must also remember that His heart is crushed by *all* those who are living in the far country, whether they are living in mud- or fur-lined pigsties. He wants them to come home. And He watches for them daily, straining to catch a glimpse of them on the horizon, ready to hike up His robe and run to them, impervious to the scandal His gracious welcome may bring.

And that is exactly what He wants from us: not dutiful obedience as we labor in His fields, cultivating our grudges and tending our self-pity, but mutual suffering as we yearn for the return of the prodigals. He calls us, not to condemn and shun, but to pray and watch, peering anxiously down the road, poised to sprint to their side and gather them up in a welcoming embrace the moment we catch a glimpse of them on the horizon.

For that, after all, is the heart of the ministry of reconciliation, which, as we saw earlier, is the ministry to which we all have been called. It is the heart that heeds the voice of God and chooses life no matter the cost. It is the heart of modeling a you-first life in a me-first world.

Making It Personal

1. Describe your own return from the pigsty to the Father. What was your initial reaction when you realized the Father not only welcomed you home but He had been waiting and watching for your return all along?_____

_____

_____

_____

_____

_____

_____

_____

_____

_____

2. Since your return to the Father, when have you allowed your heart to harden and wander back to the pigsty? How do you feel realizing that your wanderings crushed the Father's heart?_____

_____

_____

_____

_____

_____

_____

_____

_____

_____

_____

3. What areas of your life hold you back from becoming like the Father, readily forgiving and welcoming home all who repent, regardless of the depth and depravity of the pigsty from which they have come? _____

_____

_____

_____

_____

_____

_____

_____

_____

_____

_____

4. Reread the story of the prodigal son, focusing on the words in Luke 15:22–24. Pray for those you know who are wandering from the heart of God._____

_____

_____

_____

_____

_____

_____

_____

_____

_____

_____

_____

6

Pursuing God's Heart

The LORD has sought for Himself a man after His own heart.
—1 Samuel 13:14

I remember when I took my granddaughter, Brittney, then 7, to the cemetery to check on the marker of a recently deceased relative. As we looked at some of the nearby grave sites, we noticed the marker of a woman who had lived to be 102. "Wow," Brittney exclaimed, her brown eyes opening wide. "She was ready!" Needless to say, I had a good chuckle over that. But it also gave me an opportunity to talk with Brittney about being "ready" and about the way people will remember us once we're gone.

Although a visit to the cemetery may not be cheerful, it certainly can help us put things in perspective and assess our priorities. It can challenge unbelievers to reexamine their unbelief, to consider God's claim on their life, to get "ready" to leave this world. But what does it say to the believer? How does it challenge those of us who consider ourselves ready? How will we be remembered by those we leave behind? The answer lies in how we perceive ourselves while we're still here.

Identity Crisis

Every so often the familiar and somewhat predictable amnesia scenario is resurrected for another made-for-TV-movie or sitcom. The actor stares blankly into once-loved faces and professes no recognition whatsoever. Places, sounds, smells, even names—nothing seems familiar. The character's memory is gone and her sense of identity with it.

And that is exactly what has happened to us, all of us. We have lost our memory. Like the older son in the previous chapter, we have forgotten who we are and where we came from. But the forgetting goes beyond the pigsty from which the Father rescued us. It extends back to the beginning—to a time when our identity was secure in our fellowship with the Father.

Before the Rebellion...

Before the Fall...

Before the Exile...

As a result, our world is in the midst of an ongoing identity crisis. We walk around, day after day, year after year, generation after generation, trying to find our way back to... somewhere... hoping that when we get there, someone will recognize us and tell us who we are.

The problem is, even if we figure out where that "somewhere" is, we cannot get ourselves back there. That somewhere is the Garden. It calls to us from the deepest recesses of our heart. Our homesickness almost overwhelms us at times, beckoning us... to the Garden, where we once lived, even if only in the loins of Adam. To the Garden, where we once walked in intimate fellowship with our Father in the cool of the evening. To the Garden, where we once had dominion over the plants and the animals and the birds. To the Garden, where sin had no place and death did not reign... and hard hearts were unknown.

But we made a choice to go our own way, And so, we had to leave. As beautiful and as perfect as it was, we stubbornly and rebelliously packed our bags and chose to leave, to run away, to do our own thing, go our own way, run our own lives, to be the masters of our own fate. And now, like the foolish six-year-old who leaves home with nothing more than a baseball glove and a peanut-butter-and-jelly sandwich, we find ourselves adrift in the dark night, the cold wind whistling down our necks as we shiver, wondering if we will discover who we are and where we came from...before it's too late.

The terrible truth is we can't get back to the Garden. When we left the Garden, the Father stationed angels to guard the entrance. No one can return. Sin and misery and death are here to stay. Sadly, millions have tried to do the impossible, using any means at their disposal—drugs, alcohol, sex, money, power, education, success, religion, other people.

But we can return to the Father. And that relationship is really what we want and need.

No, we can't go back to the Garden. God Himself is the one who banned us from the Garden as a result of our rebellion, and He has made no provision in this life for us to return to that Garden. But we can return to the Father. And that relationship is really what we want and need. Out of His great love for us, the Father has made a way. "For God so loved the world that He gave His only begotten Son, that whoever believes in Him should not perish but have everlasting life" (John 3:16). Jesus further states that there is only one way back to the Father: "I am the way, the truth, and the life. No one comes to the Father except through Me."

John beautifully summarizes this good news again in his first epistle:

> *In this the love of God was manifested toward us, that God has sent His only begotten Son into the world, that we might live through Him. In this is love, not that we loved God, but that He loved us and sent His Son to be the propitiation for our sins.*
> —1 John 4:9–10

Jesus, God's only Son, became the propitiation, or atoning sacrifice, for our sins. As a visual demonstration of the mercy of God, Jesus paid the required price of death for our sins and bought reconciliation with our Creator. Once again, we can walk in intimate relationship with our Father in the cool of the evening. Once again, we can experience the joy of being in His presence. But not on our terms—only on His.

What futile games we play when we try to find out who we are without first returning to God or when we try to return to the Garden rather than to the Father. For without the Father, the Garden would be nothing more than hell itself.

But what about those of us who have already returned to the Father? Have we discovered who we are? Or are we, like the prodigal's older brother, still laboring on the outskirts of the Father's house, lost in an identity crisis, even as the One who loves us unconditionally beckons us to come inside?

In Bruce Demarest's *Satisfy Your Soul*, I found this quote from Henri Nouwen:

> *"One way to express the spiritual crisis of our time is to say that most of us have an address but cannot be found there. We know where we belong, but we keep being pulled away in many directions, as if we were still homeless."*
> —*Making All Things New*

Treasures of the Heart

Speaking through the prophet Samuel, God referred to David as a "man after [My] own heart" (1 Samuel 13:14). What an honor! Wouldn't it be wonderful if, years from now, someone came across your grave—or mine—and read this inscription on the headstone: *Here lies a woman [or man] after God's own heart*? What better epitaph could anyone hope for?

But is it such an unattainable legacy, reserved only for a beloved king of Israel—or is it the declaration that God longs to make over each of His children? I believe it is a description that should readily identify each and every one of us who has been born again by the Spirit of God. But is it? Sadly, I don't think so.

Why? Because, like the prodigal's older brother, we have not been honest about the treasures of our heart. Jesus said,

> *"Do not lay up for yourselves treasures on earth, where moth and rust destroy and where thieves break in and steal; but lay up for yourselves treasures in heaven, where neither moth nor rust destroys and where thieves do not break in and steal. For where you treasure is, there your heart will be also."*
> —Matthew 6:19–21

Let's look again at the story of the loving father and his two sons. The greed and selfishness in the younger son is obvious. But what of the older son? Just how greedy and selfish was he, and how callously did he disregard his father's feelings?

We often miss the fact that the older son cared no more for his father's broken heart than did the younger. When the younger son demands his inheritance, the older brother's silence betrays his hardened, self-serving nature. The original listeners to Jesus's story would have been as shocked by the behavior of the older brother as by that of the younger. In the culture of the day, where family relationships were highly esteemed, the oldest son was expected to take the position of mediator during a family crisis. The older brother in the parable had a responsibility and an obligation to seek to bring reconciliation between his father and brother, but he did not. Why?

The answer is as simple as it is sad: The older brother cared more about securing his own portion of the inheritance than he did about the broken relationship between his father and brother. By doing nothing to bring reconciliation to the situation, the older brother assured himself that the remaining two-thirds of his father's inheritance would pass immediately to him, safe from the younger brother or anyone else.

For according to Jewish custom, upon the father's death, two-thirds of the inheritance would go to the older brother as the right of the firstborn. But when the younger brother demanded and received his portion prior to his father's death, the timing of the inheritance changed. Much of the father's estate was in land, so giving the younger son his inheritance early was not a simple matter of withdrawing the necessary amount from the bank. This transaction required liquidating properties in an amount sufficient to give the younger son his share in cash. Out of necessity, this meant the older son would immediately acquire the remaining two-thirds of the estate. By remaining silent when the younger son demanded his inheritance, the older son secured for himself an early inheritance as well, although in a more respectable manner than his younger brother because he honored the Jewish custom of allowing his father to remain on the land and to oversee the estate's operation until his death.

Restoring Relationships

Though the older son appeared to honor his father by honoring Jewish custom, in reality he had dishonored him by placing his own selfish desires above his family's broken relationship. In addition to making no attempt to heal the severed family relationship, the older son sought to perpetuate the breakup by refusing to rejoice in his brother's return. As the older brother had toiled in the fields, the roots of bitterness and selfishness had grown deeper by the day, finally manifesting themselves in his accusatory words toward his father, who wanted only that his older son should rejoice with him over the prodigal's return.

> *The older brother's sin is not unique. At the root of every sin is a broken relationship— first with our heavenly Father, then with others.*

The older brother's sin is not unique. At the root of every sin is a broken relationship—first with our heavenly Father, then with others. That is the reason the Jewish festival of *Yom Kippur*, as well as the ten high holy days or "days of awe" preceding it, are the most reverent and crucial of the entire Jewish year.

Barney Kasdan's insightful book *God's Appointed Times* provides excellent background on this holy day. Once a year, up until the destruction of the Temple in A.D. 70, on *Yom Kippur* (Day of Atonement), the high priest would enter the Holy of Holies to present a blood sacrifice to atone for the sins of the people of Israel (Leviticus 23:26–32). Israel's relationship with God was thus restored and sealed for that time. Each year, the sacrifice had to be repeated.

It is important to note, as Kasdan does, that there was also an aspect of interpersonal forgiveness and restoration surrounding this holiday. During the ten days preceding *Yom Kippur*, following the blowing of the *shofars* (rams' horns) on *Rosh Hashanah* (Jewish New Year), the people were to examine their hearts to see if they held any unforgiveness against anyone. If so, they were to go to that person and extend forgiveness immediately in order for the relationship to be restored. If they hardened their hearts and refused to reconcile with their fellow Israelites, how could they expect God to forgive them when the high priest offered the sacrifice on *Yom Kippur*?

We know, of course, that the annual blood sacrifice on *Yom Kippur* is no longer needed, because Jesus, the perfect, once-for-all Sacrifice, has shed His blood for us. He writes the names of all who receive Him into the Book of Life forever, and our relationship with the Father is permanently restored. However, the principle of extending forgiveness and seeking to restore broken relationships with others in order that we might be forgiven and restored to relationship with God has not changed. Jesus said, "For if you forgive men their trespasses, your heavenly Father will also forgive you. But if you do not forgive men their trespasses, neither will your Father forgive your trespasses" (Matthew 6:14–15).

Jesus was not introducing a new concept to the people when He made these statements. He was simply reiterating what they already knew from their observance of *Yom Kippur* and the high holy days. Unforgiveness is a fatal sin, and it flourishes in the soil of a hard heart, perpetuating broken relationships and opening the door to every other imaginable sin. Broken relationships began in the Garden, but God Himself modeled the pattern for dealing with such a tragedy: He gave us Jesus. Forgiveness extended to the offender at great cost. A you-first offer of love from the wounded party. A willingness to give all for someone who deserves nothing. A recognition that a broken relationship is spawned in hell, but healed in self-sacrifice.

And it seems self-sacrifice was not something the older son was willing to consider. Instead, he pretended that he was a dutiful son, that he was more righteous than his brother, that he served his father with respect and humility. But it was all a facade because he was not honest about the treasures of his heart. While not openly defying his father like his younger brother, he was still storing up earthly treasures for himself.

However, before we condemn the older brother, consider if we are any different. Does our identity line up with that of King David? Are we men and women seeking after God's own heart, storing up treasures in heaven? Or are we, like the prodigal's older brother, playing a part, hiding silently behind a mask of respectability, serving ourselves and, in the process, forgetting our true identity?

In order to answer those questions, we must first examine the location of our treasures. Are we laying up treasures for ourselves here on earth, treasures that have no eternal value and will fade away with time? Or are we laying up treasures in heaven that, when we stand before the judgment seat of Christ, will withstand the trial of fire?

Of course, I'm not talking here about the simple giving of tithes and offerings to our local congregation or other ministries. Laying up treasures in heaven involves the relinquishing to God of every aspect of our lives, including our finances.

Acknowledging Our Source

Let's look at more of what Jesus had to say about treasures:

> *"The lamp of the body is the eye. If therefore your eye is good, your whole body will be full of light. But if your eye*

is bad [evil], your whole body will be full of darkness. If therefore the light that is in you is darkness, how great is that darkness."
—Matthew 6:22–23

In some study Bibles these two verses are separated from the preceding and following verses, almost as if the commentators didn't quite know what to do with them since, on the surface, they don't seem to relate to the surrounding text. But if we understand the setting in which these verses were spoken, they relate perfectly. In fact, they tie all the other verses together.

When Jesus spoke these words, He was using a Jewish idiom of the day. As surely as we today understand that the admonition to "keep an eye out" is a warning to be watchful and not a directive to physically pluck out an eye, so Jesus's followers understood what He meant when He spoke of a good eye and a bad/evil eye. "'If your eye is good' is an idiomatic way of saying in Hebrew, 'if you are generous,'" according to David Bivin and Roy Blizzard Jr. in *Understanding the Difficult Words of Jesus.*

> *Jesus was saying that if a person is generous with his money or treasure (having a good eye), he will be generous in all things.*

Jesus was saying that if a person is generous with his money or treasure (having a good eye), he will be generous in all things. But if a person is stingy with his money (having an evil eye), he will be stingy or selfish in all the other areas of life. And this goes far beyond tithing, or even giving to God over and above a tithe. Having a good eye means being willing to turn over our treasures not only to God but also to our fellow man—even to those who are seemingly undeserving, if God so directs. And that can sometimes be more difficult. But it is impossible to have a good eye toward God if we have an evil eye toward others.

But whoever has this world's goods, and sees his brother in need, and shuts up his heart from him, how does the love of God abide in him? My little children, let us not love in word or in tongue, but in deed and in truth.
—1 John 3:17–18

We can never have a heart like God's if we are not willing to give of ourselves to others, whether that giving involves our material treasures, our time and talents, or the offer of forgiveness and the seeking of restored relationship.

When a rich young ruler approached Jesus and asked Him what he had to do to receive eternal life, Jesus answered, "Keep the commandments." The young man responded that he had done that all his life. Jesus then said, "If you want to be perfect, go, sell what you have and give to the poor, and you will have treasure in heaven; and come, follow Me" (Matthew 19:21). And then we read one of the saddest verses in the Bible: "But when the young man heard that saying, he went away sorrowful, for he had great possessions" (v. 22).

What a tragedy! This young man, who believed he had kept the commandments throughout his lifetime, and, therefore, should qualify for eternal life, was not willing to relinquish that which he could not keep in order to gain that which he could not lose. His earthly treasures proved to be his true priority. He had no room in his heart to love God if it meant he also had to love others by giving from his "great possessions." Relationship with God and others would just have to take a backseat to his self-serving, me-first lifestyle. How clearly the young man demonstrates the truth of Jesus's words: "Where your treasure is, there your heart will be also." And how foolish we are if we think we can lay up treasures on earth and in heaven at the same time, for Jesus clearly says, "No one can serve two masters; for either he will hate the one and love the other, or else he will be loyal to the one and despise the other. You cannot serve God and mammon" (Matthew 6:24).

Jesus teaches that if we are stingy toward God and others with our financial resources, we are stingy in every aspect of our lives.

We're kidding ourselves if we think we are serving God. But if we are generous in our giving, putting God and others ahead of ourselves, then we serve God faithfully in all that we do.

Content in Him

And so, once again, we come back to heart attitude. Where are our treasures? Do we have an evil eye, clutching our treasures to ourselves, foolishly trying to hang on to that which we cannot keep, refusing to let go and invest in that which we cannot lose? Or do we have a good eye, holding our treasures in open hands, gratefully recognizing the source from which they came and the purpose for which they were given? Our answer to these questions will dictate our understanding of the next verses:

> *"Therefore I say to you, do not worry about your life, what you will eat or what you will drink; nor about your body, what you will put on. Is not life more than food and the body more than clothing?"... "Therefore do not worry, saying, 'What shall we eat?' or 'What shall we drink?' or 'What shall we wear?' For after all these things the Gentiles seek. For your heavenly Father knows that you need all these things. But seek first the kingdom of God and His righteousness, and all these things shall be added to you."*
> —Matthew 6:25,31–33

If we have an evil eye, clutching our treasures to ourselves, then we are not seeking first God's kingdom. We are seeking first our own welfare, seeing ourselves as the provider and owner of our treasures. But if we

With the proper perspective, there will be no room for worry in our lives.

have a good eye and are holding our treasures with an open hand and a grateful heart, then we are seeking first God's kingdom, recognizing Him as the provider and owner of our treasures. What greater contrast can there be between a me-first mind-set and a you-first life? With the proper perspective, there will be no room for worry in our lives. We won't be grasping to gain or hold on to fleeting treasures, but rather we will be seeking to lay up eternal riches in heaven.

A heart after God's own heart is one that seeks first His kingdom and His righteousness, leaving temporal needs in the hands of a loving and faithful Master. As long as King David walked in trust, he truly was a man after God's own heart. But his eye turned evil when he sought to satisfy his desires without regard for God's commands. It is the height of greed when a man, who has at his command an unlimited number of beautiful women, chooses to use his position to appropriate the wife of one of his own foot soldiers and then has the soldier killed in an attempt to hide his sin. David traded the joy of intimacy with God for the emptiness of stolen passion. He chose earthly rather than heavenly treasures. And he and his family paid a terrible price (see 2 Samuel 11–12).

He chose the temporal over the eternal, satisfying his sinful nature, immersing himself in darkness. Still, when the prophet Nathan confronted the king with his sin, David readily confessed and threw himself on God's mercy. He recognized the only sacrifices acceptable to God are a broken spirit and a contrite heart, the kind of heart that is content in God alone. Psalm 23 says it so plainly:

The LORD is my shepherd; I shall not want.
He makes me to lie down in green pastures; He leads me
beside the still waters.
He restores my soul; He leads me in the paths of
righteousness for His name's sake.
—Psalm 23:1–3

What a contrast between David, the humble psalmist, content to dwell in the house of the Lord forever, and David, the king, who forgot his Source and sought passing earthly pleasures.

The Disciple Jesus Loved

So what does all this have to do with our identity? Everything. David, the gentle shepherd turned warrior-king, had forgotten who he was and whence he came. He failed to put God first and tried to get himself back to the Garden, or at least his fleeting, twisted version of it. But instead of ending up smelling like roses, he found himself in a weed patch full of thorns and thistles—a powerful lesson we all can take to heart.

The Apostle John discovered the secret to maintaining a clear identity. Like King David, he truly was a man after God's heart, so much so that he could describe himself in the following words: "Now there was leaning on Jesus' bosom one of His disciples, whom Jesus loved" (John 13:23).

Most of us know that the Last Supper scene wasn't at all like many of the paintings we see hanging in churches or on dining room walls. Jesus and His disciples were observing the beginning of Passover by partaking of the *Seder* meal. And they were not sitting in chairs, lined up on one side of a long table, posing for their portrait. They were lounging on the floor, perhaps on cushions, around a low table. John, generally believed to be the youngest of the disciples, was one of the inner three, those disciples, including Peter and James, considered to be most intimate with Jesus. He was reclining beside Jesus, his head possibly even resting on Jesus's chest.

Now, when you lean up against or rest on someone's "bosom" or chest, what do you hear? A heartbeat, right? When John leaned up against Jesus's chest, he had put himself in a position to hear the very heartbeat of the Son of God. Now that is truly a man after God's own heart! And throughout the Gospel of John, the author refers to himself as "the disciple Jesus loved." Never in that Gospel account does he refer to himself other than in the third person, and always as one whose identity was centered on Jesus's love for him.

By the time John wrote his Gospel, he was quite clear on his identity: He was the disciple Jesus loved. It was no longer important to identify himself as a fisherman or the son of Zebedee or the younger brother of James; he was simply the disciple Jesus loved. It was that clear-cut identity that sustained him in persecution and tribulation, including his exile on the isle of Patmos. And, I believe, it was that identity that drew him continually into God's presence, where, "in the Spirit," he received from the Lord what we now know as the Revelation of Jesus Christ, the final book of the Bible.

John's heart was in tune with Jesus's heart. He listened to Jesus. He learned from Him. He walked with Him, talked with Him, loved Him and did so all the more after His death and resurrection. There is, after all, no other way to quell that universal longing, that homesickness that haunts each one of us. We must learn to live as John lived, seeking after God, with our ear pressed up against His bosom, listening to His heartbeat, learning from Him, walking with Him, talking with Him, storing up our treasures with Him and above all, loving Him and others with a tender, guarded heart—a good heart.

In what is known as the parable of the sower, Jesus refers to those who produce a bumper crop for God's kingdom as having a good heart (Luke 8:15). This was a common term and one rich in meaning to the Messiah's listeners. A conversation recorded between Johanan ben Zachai, a famous first-century Jewish teacher, and several of his students provides evidence of that:

> He [Johanan ben Zachai] used to say to them: Go and see which is the good way to which a person should cleave?
> R. Eliezer [b. Horkenos] said, A good eye.
> R. Joshua [ben Hananiah] said, A good associate.
> R. Jose [the Priest] said, A good neighbor.
> R. Simeon [b. Nathanel] said, One who sees the event.
> R. Eleazar b. Arach said, A good heart.
> He said to them I approve of Eleazar ben Arach more than your words, for in his words are included yours.
> —Abot 2:13 (as quoted in Brad Young's *The Parables*)

The point is that a person with a good heart will naturally also have a good eye (be kind and generous), be a good associate and a good neighbor (honor personal relationships), and see things from God's perspective (see or understand the event from a heavenly viewpoint). In other words, the ideal disciple is one with a good heart, for a good heart encompasses all that is important. According to the parable Jesus told, a disciple with a good heart enables the miracle of growth to take place, in his own life and in the lives of others.

> *According to the parable Jesus told, a disciple with a good heart enables the miracle of growth to take place, in his own life and in the lives of others.*

To be a man or woman after God's own heart is to fulfill the Great Commandment to love God with every part of our being and to love others as ourselves. It is to seek first God's kingdom and His righteousness, knowing that He will add to us whatever we need. It is to lay up treasures in heaven rather than on earth, serving God and others rather than self. It is to have a good eye, generous and full of light, rather than an evil eye, stingy and full of darkness. It is to obey God by choosing life and blessing rather than death and cursing. It is to know at the very core of our being, with every beat of our heart, with every breath we take, that He is everything—and we are loved by Him. It is to be able to say, along with David and John, that because we are the disciples Jesus loves: "Surely goodness and mercy shall follow me all the days of my life; And I will dwell in the house of the LORD forever" (Psalm 23:6).

I hope those words, along with the inscription, *A woman after God's own heart*, will one day grace my own headstone. And when some little girl reads them long after I'm gone, she will be able to declare with confidence, "Wow! She was ready!"

Making It Personal

1. Consider those you know who are not ready to leave this earth and face their Maker. How might a change in your own heart condition affect their attitude toward God?

_____

_____

_____

_____

_____

_____

_____

_____

_____

_____

2. What treasures of your heart need to be released to God?

_____

_____

_____

_____

_____

_____

_____

_____

_____

_____

_____

_____

3. How will centering your identity in being a disciple whom Jesus loves change the way you think of yourself?

_____

_____

_____

_____

_____

_____

_____

_____

_____

_____

_____

_____

4. Read Matthew 6:22–23. Do you have a good eye? Are you generous with your time, talents, and possessions?

_____

_____

_____

_____

_____

_____

_____

_____

_____

_____

_____

_____

Attitude Adjustments

My son, do not despise the chastening of the LORD, Nor detest His correction; For whom the LORD loves He corrects, Just as a father the son in whom he delights.
—Proverbs 3:11–12

Like most grandmothers, I consider my grandchildren to be the cutest and smartest that ever graced God's earth. But on occasion, I must admit I've seen in them that sin nature we all have.

I remember quite clearly the first time I was present when my son Michael had to discipline my grandson Mikey, who, at that time, was still a preschooler. I don't remember many details, like the nature of the infraction, but I do remember that it became quite a battle of the wills between my two favorite Michaels. My son ultimately triumphed, not so much because his will was stronger, but because he was bigger.

To Michael's credit, he first tried to deal with the situation by speaking firmly to Mikey. When neither that nor a time-out in the corner brought the desired results, he took his little son by the hand and said, "I'm sorry, Mikey, but I think we're going to have to go to your room for an attitude adjustment." The wailing and tears began before they ever reached Mikey's bedroom, then escalated immediately afterward. Finally, all was quiet, as father and son hugged and discussed the situation. When Michael returned, it was with a much more cooperative child in tow.

We all know about attitude adjustments, don't we? We remember getting them as children and, if we're parents, giving them as adults. But the toughest ones for me are the ones I get from my heavenly Father. And yet, they are necessary, aren't they? On occasion, like Mikey, I have stiffened my neck and vainly pitted my will against my Father's, until He had no choice but to take me to my room for an attitude adjustment. And, oh, how I wept and wailed at the seeming injustice of it! But when it was over, my Father had a much more compliant child in tow, and I had a whole new appreciation for the protective hand that held mine. As the wise King Solomon pointed out in our opening verses from Proverbs, God is a Father who loves His children enough to instruct and correct them.

Confrontations

The history of the world is about confrontation: evil vs. good; sin vs. righteousness; tyranny vs. freedom; man vs. God. Although Jesus already won the ultimate victory on the cross and sealed it with His resurrection, the enemies of God continue to harass His children. And many of us are weary from these ongoing skirmishes. We're anxious for our King's return and the ensuing victory celebration. But until that happens, confrontation will continue to be a way of life, no matter how hard we try to avoid it.

> *God is peeling away the layers of sin and death in our lives, and sometimes it hurts.*

Becoming a Christian does not free a person from confrontation. In fact it does the opposite. Not only do we face opposition from the devil, we also find ourselves in a direct line of confrontation with God Himself. God is peeling away the layers of sin and death in our lives, and sometimes it hurts. When we said yes to Jesus as our Savior, we said yes to God's working of His Spirit within us: "But we all, with unveiled face, beholding as in a mirror the glory of the Lord, are being transformed into the same image from glory to glory, just as by the Spirit of the Lord" (2 Corinthians 3:18).

God, through the working of His Spirit within us, is in the process of changing us into His own image. Pretty amazing, isn't it? Fallen, fallible, foolish mortals that we are, we will one day mirror the very image of God. And what does that image look like? Jesus said, "He who has seen Me has seen the Father" (John 14:9).

And so, we have the promise that we will one day look like Jesus. Does that mean we will physically look like He did when He walked the earth? Or even that we will look like the risen, majestic Jesus who appeared to John in the Book of Revelation?

I believe Scripture is referring to a spiritual image rather than a physical one. We are, after all, spiritual beings. And, though we will someday have new bodies, even as Jesus did after His resurrection, the meaning of the Scripture runs much deeper than that. Being changed into His image means that God, starting with the planting of His incorruptible seed within us at the time of our new birth (see 1 Peter 1:23), is forming or "growing" the image of His Son in us (He must increase and we must decrease [see John 3:30]), much the same way that the baby Jesus grew in Mary's womb from the seed planted there by God's Spirit. What an awesome promise!

But how does God do that? How does He take us through those steps of change from what we once were to what He has promised we will become? By confrontation or, more precisely, by a series of confrontations.

In the beginning, those confrontations are usually obvious ones: If we have been involved in blatant sin and destructive habits prior to our conversion—crime, addictions, immoral relationships—God will either effect an immediate deliverance within us or bring us, through various circumstances, to a place where we are ready and willing to let those things go. Then, once those obvious outward sins are dealt with, comes the hard part: He begins to confront our attitudes. From that point on, attitude adjustments are inevitable. And we never outgrow the need for them.

Unrealistic Expectations?

In his famous discourse known as the Sermon on the Mount, Jesus focused on attitude adjustments, shining His light into the hearts of men and women. I believe this can be seen in Matthew 5:20: "For I say to you, that unless your righteousness exceeds the righteousness of the scribes and Pharisees, you will by no means enter the kingdom of heaven" (see also 5:21–39). Jesus was indeed addressing the people's behavior, but He was also going deeper, confronting their attitudes—their heart condition.

For years the people had lived with a perversion of the teachings given to Moses by God on Mount Sinai. For years their religious leaders, with the intention of protecting God's Word and preventing the people from sinning, had taken the existing commands of God and added to them their own teachings and requirements. And for years the people had labored under the misconception that keeping these commands was God's required means of salvation. That was bad enough. Now they were hearing that it was not sufficient to keep God's commands outwardly—they must keep them inwardly as well! Given the condition of the human heart, it must indeed have seemed a hopeless situation.

> *The* Torah *was given to those who were already accepted by God so they would know the family rules and walk in such a way as to honor God and draw the other nations to Him.*

When God's *Torah* ("teachings" or "instructions"; later translated "law") was first given to Moses, the people understood that it was given as a guideline for how they were to live—or, as the Hebrew word *halakhah* better describes it, how they were to walk as God's chosen people. Because of God's promise to their forefathers, the Israelites knew they were already God's chosen ones. And because God had already brought them out of the bondage of Egypt (a picture of salvation from the bondage of sin in the world), they were already saved because of what God had done. The *Torah* was given to those who were already accepted by

God so they would know the family rules and walk in such a way as to honor God and draw the other nations to Him.

As a parent, I did not wait until my children learned to walk to grant them admission into the family. They were mine from the moment of conception, and there was nothing they could do to sever that familial relationship. Nevertheless, once they were born into the family, their father and I had a responsibility to teach them how to walk, in more ways than one. There was, of course, the physical walking they had to learn, which included a lot of falls, a lot of tears, and a lot of patience. But teaching children to walk in godliness is a lot more difficult, a lot more time-consuming, and includes a lot more falls, tears, and patience.

Originally, biblical Israel understood they were already God's chosen people, that He had redeemed them from Egypt, and that He had even provided a sacrificial system to atone for their sins when they did fall. But they began to presume on His grace and mercy. They forgot that, although they were saved by grace, there is still a law of sowing and reaping that even the sacrificial system does not override.

And so, despite countless warnings to repent and return to the walk prescribed by God for His chosen people, they continued in sin, walking more and more in the ways of their idolatrous neighbors until they eventually ended up in exile in Babylon. However, because they were still God's chosen people and because His love for them was so great, He eventually brought back a remnant to their own land. (Many chose to stay in Babylon, because it seemed easier to remain than to return and try to eke out a living in the broken down rubble that once was Jerusalem.)

The remnant that returned should have learned their lesson. But had they? Seemingly not, as their attitudes soon changed. Maybe they decided that since not walking according to God's law had gotten them into such trouble, they would now focus on keeping every jot and tittle of His commands in an effort to earn their way back into the fold of God's chosen people. Or maybe it was pride in being those chosen people that caused them to overemphasize the finer points of the law. Either way, the *Torah*, which God had originally given as loving instructions and guidelines for His chosen people, they now began to pervert into a legalistic system of behavior-oriented salvation.

They still weren't getting it. If they had not already been God's chosen people, He would not have rescued them from bondage in the first place. Now they were futilely trying to earn what God had already given them as a gift. In so doing, they missed what God truly wanted from them: to love Him with all their heart, soul, mind, and strength, and to love their neighbor as themselves.

So, we return, once again, to attitudes—heart conditions—the primary topic of the Sermon on the Mount. Was Jesus calling the people to unrealistic expectations, impossible requirements? Or was He confronting the perversion of *Torah*—God's loving instructions for His children—into a legalistic system of works? Was He simply challenging God's people, once and for all, to learn and practice *halakhah* as it was meant to be?

To "Fill" or "Fulfill" *Torah*?

In most translations of Matthew 5:17, the common Greek word *plerôsai* is translated "to fulfill," which can lead to the theological implication that Jesus obeyed every command of *Torah*, therefore, completing or ending it so that no one else need observe it. However, in my view, this presents a real problem because in that same verse, Jesus said, "Do not think that I came to destroy the Law or the Prophets." If He did not come to destroy the law, why would He then say He had fulfilled it so no one else need follow it—in essence, nullifying the very law that He just said He did not come to destroy?

One possible explanation, which I favor, lies in another common translation of that Greek word, which is "to fill," not "to fulfill." This translation paints Christ's statement in a slightly different light and lines up with the previous statement. Messianic Jewish scholar and translator David Stern believes the meaning of Matthew 5:17 is more along these lines: Don't think that I have come to abolish the *Torah* or the Prophets. I have come not to abolish but to complete.

Further, in the *Complete Jewish Bible*, Stern comments regarding the verse:

> *My view is that Yeshua [Jesus] came not to* fulfill, *but to* fill *the* Torah *and the ethical pronouncements of the Prophets* full *with their* complete meaning, *so that everyone can know all that obedience entails.... In fact, this is the theme of the entire Sermon on the Mount; and* Mattityahu *[Matthew] 5:17, understood in this way, is its theme sentence; for Yeshua goes on from there to give specifics. Interestingly, this understanding is concordant with Jewish tradition, which says that when the Messiah comes he will both explain obscure passages of* Torah *and actually change it.*

In addition, authors David Bivin and Roy Blizzard Jr. in *Understanding the Difficult Words of Jesus*, elaborate on the meanings of the words *destroy* and *fulfill* as they pertain to the above Scriptures:

> *"Destroy" and "fulfill" are technical terms used in rabbinic argumentation. When a sage felt that a colleague had misinterpreted a passage of Scripture, he would say, "You are destroying the Law!" Needless to say, in most cases his colleague strongly disagreed. What was "destroying the Law" for one sage, was "fulfilling the Law" (correctly interpreting Scripture) for another.*
>
> *What we see in Matthew 5:17 ff. is a rabbinic discussion. Someone has accused Jesus of "destroying" the Law. Of course, neither Jesus nor his accuser would ever think of literally destroying the Law. Furthermore, **it would never enter the accuser's mind to charge Jesus with intent to abolish part or all of the Mosaic Law. What is being called into question is Jesus's system of interpretation, the way he interprets Scripture.***

When accused, Jesus strongly denies that his method of interpreting Scripture "destroys" or weakens its meaning. He claims, on the contrary, to be more orthodox than his accuser. For Jesus, a "light" commandment ("Do not bear hatred in your heart") is as important as a "heavy" commandment ("Do not murder"). And a disciple who breaks even a "light" commandment will be considered "light" (have an inferior position) in Jesus's movement (Matthew 5:19)" (emphasis added).

This possible confusion between "to fill" and "to fulfill," as well as a lack of understanding of the Hebrew usage of "to fulfill" and "to destroy" in rabbinic discussion, fuel what I believe to be a common misconception: that Christians should not be concerned with *Torah* because the Law has already been "fulfilled" (finished and done away with) and thus no longer need be observed. Again, we know that we are saved by grace and not by keeping *Torah*. But as we saw earlier in this chapter, the nation of Israel was also saved or delivered from Egypt by grace, prior to the giving of *Torah*. The Law was given after their deliverance as a means of teaching what God expected from them as His chosen people.

Now let's apply this to where we are today. As Christians, we know we are saved by grace, kept by grace, delivered by grace, accepted by grace—in essence, we have no other standing before God except grace. How foolish we would be if we tried to earn what God has already freely given us! We would be as foolish as the Israelite remnant God graciously brought back from captivity in Babylon, who then tried to earn their way back into the elite circle of His chosen people by perverting His teachings into a legalistic system.

> *How foolish we would be if we tried to earn what God has already freely given us!*

On the other hand, we would be just as foolish to toss out His teachings—the *Torah* of the Old Testament—because we believe those teachings no longer apply to us. In fact, Romans 15:4 teaches just the opposite: "For whatever things were written before were written for our learning, that we through patience and comfort of the Scriptures might have hope." Since no other Scriptures existed except the Old Testament at the time the book of Romans was penned, and the Old Testament contained the law and teachings of God, it is obvious that they were still valid "for our learning." These laws and teachings certainly are not the means to salvation, but they are wise guidelines for *halakhah*—how we, as God's people, should walk.

Now, of course, many of these laws and statutes were peculiar to the times and culture, including the fact that Israel lived under a theocratic government. So, we probably won't glean many practical points in how to live from laws regarding mold eradication or the sacrificing of pigeons. However, the basic laws contained within what are commonly known as the Ten Commandments are not only the basis for Western civilization, they are God's timeless guidelines for healthy living, establishing and raising a family, and relating to others within our community. To abandon those teachings would be to open the door to chaos and anarchy of the worst sort.

Explaining and Completing

The understanding that Jesus came to "fill" *Torah*—to more fully and accurately interpret it—rather than do away with it, coincides with the Jewish tradition that, as David Stern writes, Messiah would "both explain obscure passages of *Torah* and actually change it." When we keep that thought in mind, we can better understand what was going on between Jesus and His listeners as He delivered His teachings in the Sermon on the Mount.

Throughout this sermon Jesus repeatedly says, "You have *heard* that it was *said*... But I say to you..." What was Jesus doing? He was not challenging the validity of God's Word, but rather the interpretations of God's Word that the people had *heard* from some of their religious leaders. He was, more specifically, correctly interpreting, explaining, and completing *Torah*; in the process, He was changing what His listeners understood it to say.

He was telling them that it was not enough to refrain from physically murdering someone; God wanted them to carry no malice or anger or resentment in their hearts toward others. He told them it wasn't enough to abstain from adultery; they must refrain from lust as well. He told them the only legitimate reason for divorce was sexual immorality. He spoke against swearing or making oaths, saying rather that their speech should be straightforward and honest. He told them not to seek revenge; to treat their enemies in a loving manner and to pray for them; to do their charitable deeds anonymously; to pray and fast humbly and unpretentiously; to forgive others so that God would forgive them. He said to lay up treasures in heaven and not on earth, and to "seek first the kingdom of God and His righteousness" (Matthew 6:33), trusting that God would then faithfully supply their physical needs. Jesus went on to warn them that if they judged others, they would be judged in turn. He told them to be faithful and diligent in prayer, expecting God to answer; to treat others as they would like to be treated; to seek the narrow, less traveled way; and to learn to discern between true and false prophets by the "fruits" their works produced.

Jesus, in the Sermon on the Mount, clarified and expounded on the way we are to walk in God's kingdom as His children. This was radical teaching. Ultimately, what He was teaching them was that *Torah* was not meant to be a legalistic system; it was given as a loving instruction manual from a wise and caring Father. If, out of love and gratitude to God, they committed themselves to walk according to His guidelines, they would find great blessings. If they chose instead to walk their own way, they would reap the inevitable consequences.

In addition, by outlining impossibly high standards for obedience, I believe Jesus wanted them to see how futile it was to try to earn their way into heaven by attempting to follow a legalistic system. At the same time, He wanted them to see God's ideal for His people, an ideal that was so far above and beyond their own thinking or strength that it would drive them to an ever-deepening dependence on God rather than themselves.

The Double Message

This radical teaching, which requires a radical attitude adjustment in order to be received, is meant to invoke a response to Christ's radical call to discipleship, which is part of the double message of the Cross. The first part of that double message is obvious: The Cross represents God's grace, His unconditional love and free gift to sinners. The price of our salvation has already been paid in full. He sees us as perfect because we are in Christ and Christ is perfect. But when we focus solely on that half of the message, we are in danger of falling into the same trap as did the Israelites prior to the Babylonian exile. We may presume upon God's grace, forgetting that there is still a prescribed way for God's children to walk out their faith. When we live this way, there are consequences, not only for ourselves, but also for the world that looks at us and sees us as hypocrites who preach one way of walking while ordering our steps according to another.

The second half of the message of the Cross is not about our salvation; it is about our discipleship, our commitment to walk as God has called us to walk, even when it requires the laying down of our own will and life (which it always does, to one degree or another). It is so easy to look at the Cross and see our precious Savior suffering for *us*, paying for *our* sins that *we* might be restored to the Father. But to go no farther in our vision and understanding of the Cross is to be stuck in selfishness and immaturity. We also need to look at the Cross and remember that Jesus said, "If anyone desires to come after Me, let him deny himself, and take up his cross, and follow Me" (Matthew 16:24). That's a pretty radical invitation, wouldn't you agree?

Jesus never said that following Him would be easy. In fact, He promised us just the opposite. He said, "In the world you will have tribulation; but be of good cheer, I have overcome the world" (John 16:33). This is why many of His followers, especially those who came simply to witness and receive His miracles, eventually turned around and went back to their old lives. Following Jesus was just too hard. And that is the same reason that many turn back from following Him today. When they realize there is more to being a Christian than simply enjoying the blessings—well, thanks, but no thanks!

At the same time, there is a danger in focusing exclusively on this second aspect of the double message of the Cross. We can become so absorbed in correctly observing God's prescribed way of living that we lose sight of the free gift of salvation. When that happens, we fall into the same trap as did the Israelites after the Babylonian exile: turning God's loving guidelines for living into a perverted system of legalism and works. This, too, has consequences, one of which is that the world looks at the church and says, "Impossible! I'd never be able to live up to such stringent requirements! And besides, why would I want to? They might talk a lot about joy, but I sure don't see any in their lives!"

> *Answering God's higher calling, to go beyond ourselves and model a you-first life to a me-first world, is no easy task.*

Answering God's higher calling, to go beyond ourselves and model a you-first life to a me-first world, is no easy task. In fact, it is an impossible one, far beyond ourselves and our own abilities, unless we grasp the balance of the Cross's double message. Without complete dependence on the One who already paid the price for our salvation, and without complete commitment to walk as He's called us to walk, it is an exercise in futility. But God, who calls us to do the impossible, is also the God who accomplishes the impossible.

Three Teachers—One Progressive Teaching

God the Father spoke to His people by giving them *Torah* through His servant Moses. These were His instructions for right living and right relationship. Then Jesus not only fully interpreted the Law, He also modeled for us this you-first way of living. Finally, the Holy Spirit was sent.

Most of us are familiar with the coming of the Holy Spirit on the day of Pentecost. But have we thought about the purpose and significance of His coming on that particular day? Why on the Feast of *Shavuot,* or Pentecost?

Shavuot means "weeks." The festival was often called *Hag ha-Shavuot*, or the Feast of Weeks (see Exodus 34:22; Deuteronomy 16:10; 2 Chronicles 8:13). This holiday was called the Feast of Weeks because seven weeks were counted from the Feast of Firstfruits until the celebration of *Shavuot*. On the Feast of Weeks, offerings from the wheat harvest were brought to the Temple, marking the end of the grain harvest. After the destruction of the Temple in A.D. 70, the focus of *Shavuot* soon shifted from an agricultural festival to the commemoration of the giving of *Torah* on Mount Sinai, since *Torah* was given in the same month, possibly on the same day (Exodus 19:1). In fact, some scholars now believe that the roots of *Shavuot*'s association with *Torah* predate the Temple's destruction and that the Jews of Jesus's day already would have been celebrating the giving of *Torah* at Pentecost, along with the harvest celebration.

With faithful Jewish men from all over the world gathered in Jerusalem for this great feast day, what more appropriate time for the Holy Spirit of God to come and empower the disciples of Jesus Christ?

When the Day of Pentecost had fully come, they were all with one accord in one place. And suddenly there came a sound from heaven, as of a rushing mighty wind, and it filled the whole house where they were sitting.

Then there appeared to them divided tongues, as of fire, and one sat upon each of them. And they were all filled with the Holy Spirit and began to speak with other tongues, as the Spirit gave them utterance.
And there were dwelling in Jerusalem Jews, devout men, from every nation under heaven. And when this sound occurred, the multitude came together, and were confused, because everyone heard them speak in his own language.
—Acts 2:1–6

The Feast of *Shavuot* or Pentecost was one of the three times each year (the Feast of Tabernacles, which occurs five days after the Day of Atonement, and Passover are the others) when Jewish men were required to journey, even from countries so far away that they spoke other languages, to Jerusalem. Although many of those who saw and heard these newly Spirit-filled believers were initially confused, about 3,000 of them believed the gospel message passionately delivered by Peter. They joined the 120 as followers of Jesus.

On the very day that Jews from everywhere were celebrating the wheat harvest and God the Father's giving of *Torah* at Mount Sinai, the Holy Spirit arrived. He is the One the Great Teacher, Jesus Christ, had said would "teach you all things, and bring to your remembrance all things that I said to you" (John 14:26). We see here a powerful meeting of the Godhead in teaching what He expects of His people. The Father, the Son, and the Spirit agree. God, speaking through the prophet Jeremiah, had predicted this very thing years earlier, when He said, "I will put My law [teachings] in their minds, and write it on their hearts; and I will be their God, and they shall be My people" (Jeremiah 31:33, author's amplification in brackets).

> *Only the Spirit can enable and empower God's people to live as powerful yet loving witnesses for Him, modeling a you-first life to a me-first world.*

God had fulfilled this great prophecy by sending His Holy Spirit to live within His people, to instruct them, remind them, and enable them to walk according to His way. But for what purpose? Jesus explained it quite clearly in Acts 1:8: "But you shall receive power when the Holy Spirit has come upon you; and you shall be witnesses to Me in Jerusalem, and in all Judea and Samaria, and to the end of the earth."

"You shall be witnesses to Me..." God sent the Holy Spirit on the Day of Pentecost for the same reason He gave *Torah* to Moses on Mount Sinai centuries earlier: to teach those who know Him how to walk in such a way that those who do not know Him would be drawn to Him as well. The Father, by giving *Torah*, taught the children of Israel how to walk; Jesus clarified and expanded *Torah* to include heart attitudes as well as actions; the Holy Spirit empowered God's people to walk accordingly. Three teachers, one teaching—yet each one added a key element in the unfolding revelation of God.

The Father gave *Torah* to govern the people's *actions*. Jesus showed the people that their *attitudes* needed to line up with God's teachings. The Holy Spirit continually confronts God's people with the *challenge* and the *choice* to walk as God has called them to walk. Only the Spirit can enable and empower God's people to live as powerful yet loving witnesses for Him, modeling a you-first life to a me-first world.

And it all starts—and ends—with some very radical attitude adjustments.

Making It Personal

1. Review the times God has confronted you with the need for an attitude adjustment. What was your first reaction?

_____

_____

_____

_____

_____

_____

_____

_____

_____

_____

2. Consider the double message of the Cross. In what ways have you embraced the salvation message while rejecting the call and cost of discipleship? _____

_____

_____

_____

_____

_____

_____

_____

_____

_____

_____

_____

3. Explain in your own words how the Father, Son, and Spirit each teach us the way we are to walk as God's children.

_____

_____

_____

_____

_____

_____

_____

_____

_____

_____

4. Read Proverbs 3:11–12 and ask God to show you if there are attitudes in your heart even now that require an adjustment—then ask Him to change your heart and enable you to have a right attitude in these situations or circumstances. _____

_____

_____

_____

_____

_____

_____

_____

_____

_____

_____

_____

8

"Abide In Me"

"I am the true vine, and My Father is the vinedresser....
"Abide in Me, and I in you. As the branch cannot bear
fruit of itself, unless it abides in the vine, neither can you,
unless you abide in Me.
"I am the vine, you are the branches. He who abides in
Me, and I in him, bears much fruit; for without Me you
can do nothing"
—John 15:1,4–5

Why is it that those of us who claim to believe God's Word have such trouble accepting what Jesus said in John 15:5, "Without Me you can do nothing"? In truth, I doubt I've ever met anyone who fully believes that statement. Oh, a lot of us claim to believe it, because we wouldn't dare call Jesus a liar. But as long as we continue trying to do things on our own, we are not putting our beliefs into practice. And that's a scary thought. Why would we commit ourselves to follow the One who claims to be Truth if we do not believe (and do) what He says?

I must admit, there are times when I catch a glimpse of the absolute truth of His statement in John 15. The realization usually occurs when I am lying flat on my face in the dirt, after attempting to do something in my own strength. But once I have allowed my heavenly Father to pick me up and comfort me for a time, sooner or later I somehow find myself again walking in my own way rather than God's, back on the old familiar path marked "I can do it!"

Ever been there? Sure you have—many times. And if you've ever raised children, you've had to pick them up from that same path each time they fell on their button noses and screamed out in frustration. Of course, being a loving and compassionate parent, as soon as you spotted those little ones heading down that path, you offered to help. "I can do it myself," the determined dynamos insisted. And off they went, only to trip over their own pint-sized egos before they'd made it very far around the track. Then it was up to you to come to the rescue.

The difference, of course, is that, physically, most children do eventually learn how to walk on their own. But when it comes to walking God's way, the only way we ever learn how to do it is to realize that we can't—not by ourselves. We need God...and we need others. For God's way, after all, is to walk in such a manner that we model a you-first life to a me-first world, which can only happen within the context of relationships. And relationships are something we simply cannot do alone.

> *We live in a pull-yourself-up-by-the-bootstraps country, but we serve a God who says, "Without me you can do nothing."*

Declaration of Independence?

We Americans are proud of our Declaration of Independence. We view it as a pronouncement of our right to govern ourselves, to be free from oppression and tyranny, and to pursue happiness in whatever way we choose, so long as we respect the rights of others and stay within the confines of our nation's laws.

But for those of us who are also Christians, this presents a dilemma. We may consider ourselves independent politically, but spiritually? Impossible. Independence is the antithesis of true spirituality and what a terrible time we have separating the two concepts. We live in a pull-yourself-up-by-the-bootstraps country, but we serve a God who says, "Without me you can do nothing."

Culturally, we may have a do-your-own-thing attitude, but as members of the church, that won't work.

We've allowed ourselves to become fragmented into countless isolated units that ironically claim to be integral parts of a united Body. We come together every week to hold hands and pray for one another, to worship God and sing of our unity in Him, and then we disperse to our *own* homes, our *own* lives, our *own* interests, even our *own* ministries. I have what's mine; you have what's yours. The problems lies not in ownership per se, but in the attitude we have toward all these things. We have been duped into thinking that we can be effective Christians while remaining independent from others. In effect, we have become body parts saying to one another, "I don't need you. I can do it myself!" The Apostle Paul, in 1 Corinthians, addresses such faulty thinking:

> *In many countries, particularly countries outside the West, believers more readily understand and live out the principles of unity and interdependence.*

> *But now indeed there are many members, yet one body. And the eye cannot say to the hand, "I have no need of you"; nor again the head to the feet, "I have no need of you." No, much rather, those members of the body which seem to be weaker are necessary. And those members of the body which we think to be less honorable, on these we bestow greater honor; and our unpresentable parts have greater modesty, but our presentable parts have no need. But God composed the body, having given greater honor to that part which lacks it, that there should be no schism in the body, but that the members should have the same care for one another.*
> —1 Corinthians 12:20–25

In many countries, particularly countries outside the West, believers more readily understand and live out the principles of unity and interdependence. They practice it regularly, sometimes out of necessity. For instance, in many countries where Christians are persecuted for their faith, it is not uncommon for families and individuals to take refuge together in one home or building, to share their provisions, and to care and pray for one another. But, most of the time, at least for many of us, interdependence is an idea so foreign to us that we give it no serious consideration in our everyday lives. Much of the problem, I believe, stems from our own arrogance, as well as a lack of appreciation for God's grace.

Perhaps because we have so many worldly goods and conveniences, and because we so fiercely pursue our own happiness and success, it is easier for us to count God's gifts as possessions we've earned in our own strength rather than as gracious blessings. That attitude is dangerous, because we can easily become stingy and judgmental toward others, rationalizing that if they worked as hard as we do, they too could amass the same possessions and conveniences that we have. Joel Belz, founder of *World* magazine, Asheville, North Carolina, sums it up this way:

If, on the one hand, we are persuaded deep in our hearts that we have earned what we have in life, then we tend to expect others to do the same. But if we know that everything we have in life is a gift, then we are inclined to extend a giving heart toward others. The tension between these two points of view is hard for American conservatives to resolve—and perhaps especially so for American conservatives who are also serious Christians.

For Christians are by biblical definition people who have come to understand that "for by grace you are saved, and not by works." And most Americans are also people whose freedom and prosperity have been all but handed to them on a silver platter. Surely, some of us have scurried and hustled—but can we really claim we've scurried and hustled more in our lives than have our counterparts in Honduras or Angola or Bangladesh? Or was it more that

we were blessed to land in a context where our scurry
and hustle paid off faster and more easily than theirs ever
will? A realistic (and humble) American will respond just
like a realistic and humble Christian. He will say it was
all of grace.
—"What Pat must prove," *World*, March 20, 1999

And that's the bottom line: It is all of grace, not of works. Therefore, everything we have is an undeserved gift, not an earned reward. When we fail to make that distinction, we give first place to our independent, Americanized attitude rather than God's higher calling to a humble, selfless, you-first life. We can be good patriotic citizens, and we can be God-honoring Christians. But we cannot preach a gospel that is tainted with materialism, isolationism, and me-first success.

People... Need People
To abide in Christ is to put Him first, making our first priority time spent with Him, learning and meditating on His Word, praying and communing with Him, listening for His response and then obeying. It also requires being in relationship with others, just as Jesus lived day in and day out with His disciples. When I hear people say they can be Christians without attending church and fellowshipping with other believers, I know they have not understood God's teachings on how we are to live as His children. To claim to follow Christ, yet to walk other than the way He walked, is impossible. In 1 John 2:6 we read, "He who says he abides in Him ought himself also to walk just as He walked."

And how was that? Jesus walked in selfless, intimate relationship with God and with others—the perfect model of a you-first life. But what about Jesus's disciples, those who walked with Him? Was their walk perfect? Hardly! And yet, His relationship with them was such that He loved them to the point of laying down His life for them. How can we ever hope to achieve that sort of walk if we are not involved in the lives of our brothers and sisters? With all the weaknesses and warts of the church, we still need to be an active part of it.

Why? Because we need each other. And because God is not enough.

Wait a minute! That sounds like...like blasphemy! How can I make such an unthinkable statement?

I didn't. God did.

In the Garden of Eden, before sin and death entered the scene, while God still walked with man in perfect communion, the Creator looked at His creation and pronounced it "very good" (Genesis 1:31)—except for one thing: man was alone (2:18).

Adam had dominion over all the animals, he had a job (to tend and keep the garden), and he had unbroken relationship with God. But God said, "That's not good, Adam. You need more. You need human relationship."

David Ferguson, author and founder of Intimate Life Ministries, in his book *The Great Commandment Principle*, describes what happened in Genesis 2:18 as "the first human crisis: Adam, needy for human relationship *by God's design*, was alone" (emphasis added).

Did you notice that phrase, "by God's design"? What does that mean? Genesis 1:27 explains it this way: "So God created man in His own image; in the image of God He created him; male and female He created them."

God, by design, created man in His own image. And God, by design, created man with the need for human relationship. Among other things, to be created in God's image is to be created with a need for human relationship. And if God created us with a need for human relationship, then it stands to reason that it is not good for us to be without those relationships.

Years ago Barbra Streisand sang a song about people needing relationship with other people. She was right. What her song did not address is the fact that, without first being in right relationship with God, we can never properly or effectively relate to people. We might know people, interact with them, use them, even procreate with them, but we are still alone, because we are not relating to them as God has purposed for us to do: *through the modeling of a you-first life to a me-first world.* Any human relationship that does not flow out of relationship with the Father does not model the One in whose image we are made. It is a selfish relationship, based on a me-first lifestyle, and does not bring us the fulfillment that God desires for us. It is focused on meeting all of our needs except the one need that God calls us to focus on: the need to give ourselves to others as we seek to meet their needs.

That is the essence of a you-first life, the sort of life Jesus modeled to us as He walked among us, being moved with compassion by the needs of others, giving Himself to them in order to meet those needs, and ultimately laying down His life in the process. And that is the higher calling to which God beckons us, a calling that transforms us from self-centered people to people focused on God and the needs of others. It is the calling to live according to the walk God has outlined in His Word, and it is the only calling that will ever bring us the fulfillment we seek.

> *And that is the higher calling to which God beckons us, a calling that transforms us from self-centered people to people focused on God and the needs of others.*

We have been called to walk as Jesus walked, to pick up our cross and follow Him, to give our lives as witnesses to the world of the One in whose image we are made. But the minute we think we can do that without being in intimate relationship with Him and with others, we have ceased to abide in Him; we have stepped off God's path and have returned to the way that God declares "not good."

The Cry of the Savior's Heart

Jesus longed to see His followers walk according to God's purpose and plan for their lives. It was, in fact, the cry of His heart, as we see in His longest recorded prayer in John 17. This prayer is often referred to as the High Priestly Prayer because, as the Great High Priest, Jesus was interceding for us.

*"I pray for them. I do not pray for the world but for those whom You have given Me, for they are Yours. And all Mine are Yours, and Yours are Mine, and I am glorified in them.... Holy Father, keep through Your name those whom You have given Me **that they may be one as We are**.... They are not of the world, just as I am not of the world.... As You sent Me into the world, I also have sent them into the world.... I do not pray for these alone, but also for those who will believe in Me through their word, **that they all may be one, as You, Father, are in Me, and I in You; that they also may be one in Us, that the world may believe that You sent Me.** And the glory which You gave Me I have given them, **that they may be one just as We are one: I in them, and You in Me; that they may be made perfect in one**, and **that the world may know that You have sent Me**, and have loved them as You have loved Me.... You loved Me before the foundation of the world.... And I have declared to them Your name, and will declare it, **that the love with which You loved Me may be in them, and I in them.**"*
—John 17:9–11,16,18,20–24,26 (emphasis added)

We see within this prayer three primary points regarding God's specified way of walking within relationships: unselfishness, unity, and witness.

In verse 10, Jesus said to His Father, "All Mine are Yours." All that the Son had—everyone God had given Him in relationship—He acknowledged as belonging to the Father. He laid no private claim to them. He didn't have to because He knew that everything the Father had was also His, because they are one. As a result, the Father and Son have a completely unselfish relationship.

Isn't that what the father was trying to get across to his older son in the story of the prodigal? When the ungrateful older son was whining because his father was throwing a party for the returning prodigal but had never thrown one for him, the father replied, "Son, you are always with me, and *all that I have is yours*" (Luke 15:31, emphasis added). We have no record that this older son ever grasped the truth of that statement, and that is the saddest part of the entire story. The son did not understand that he was always with his father and, therefore, all that his father had was his. Instead, he spent his life trying to amass his own wealth, gathering it to himself, storing it up for his own use, worrying and grumbling that he did not have enough, growing bitter and hardhearted in the process. Regardless of how much this older son ended up with, it would never be enough, for he had not learned to walk according to God's model of a you-first life in relationship to others.

> *We will be no different than the older son, thinking life is all about us and missing the joy of living for God and others.*

We need to see God's blessings—wealth, possessions, family, time, health—as priceless treasures that we steward to further His kingdom and benefit others, not as things to horde for our own pleasure. Otherwise we will never effectively model the you-first life to which God has called us. We will continue to be alone—"not good"—because our relationships will be me-centered. And, ultimately, our lives will not account for anything if we continue to disbelieve Jesus's statement that apart from Him we can do nothing. We will be no different than the older son, thinking life is all about us and missing the joy of living for God and others.

The second point in Jesus's prayer regarding relationship is unity. Unselfishness and unity are inseparable. The Father and Son were in perfect unity because all they possessed they willingly released to each other. There was no competition, no jockeying for position, no self-seeking. And that's the sort of unity that Jesus prayed His followers would achieve: "that they may be one as We are" (John 17:11).

Did Jesus think we would ever achieve that unity on our own? Of course not. That's why He told His disciples that "without Me you can do nothing" (John 15:5). He was praying to the Father to bring about this unity among all believers down through the ages. Only the Father could cause that unity to become a reality in our lives. Has it happened? Has Jesus's prayer been answered?

Not completely. At many times in history, Christians in many lands have freely and readily shared whatever resources and gifts God had given them. And today, there are gracious, giving believers who have come to realize the beauty and joy of unity among those who share a common passion for the one true God.

But overall we have not even come close to seeing the fulfillment of Christ's priestly prayer for His followers. And I can't help but believe that our selfishness and disunity grieve the heart of God.

Is there any hope for us? Will we ever experience that glorious unity among believers for which our Savior prayed? Only God can bring us to that place.

I believe Jesus gives an indication of how He will bring us together in John 16:33, just before He "lifted up His eyes to heaven" (John 17:1) and prayed for us to be in unity. He said, "In the world you will have *tribulation*; but be of good cheer, I have overcome the world" (emphasis added).

According to the *Spirit-Filled Life Bible*, edited by Jack Hayford, the word for *tribulation* in the above Scripture is the Greek word *thlipsis*, which means:

> *Pressure, oppression, stress, anguish, tribulation, adversity, affliction, crushing, squashing, squeezing, distress. Imagine placing your hand on a stack of loose items and manually compressing them. That is* thlipsis, *putting a lot of pressure on that which is free and unfettered.* Thlipsis *is like spiritual bench-pressing. The word is used of crushing grapes or olives in a press.*

Can you see now why Jesus, upon warning His followers of the coming trials, added the admonition to "be of good cheer"? Knowing that we are in for pressure, affliction, anguish, distress, crushing, squeezing, and just plain suffering, it is not likely that our immediate reaction would be one of good cheer. But, immediately following Christ's warning of sure tribulation, we find Him interceding for us, asking God to keep us from the evil one and to make us one as He and the Father are one.

We must learn to live together in unity with our brothers and sisters in Christ, one in the family of God.

I believe Jesus was indicating that our unity will only be achieved as troubles squeeze us together, binding us to one another until, at last, we realize that not only do we need God, but we also need each other. It is in tribulation that we are "made perfect in one" (John 17:23), united as are the Father and Son.

We must learn to live together in unity with our brothers and sisters in Christ, one in the family of God. It is not good for us to be alone. Alone, without God, we accomplish nothing. Alone, without human relationship, the evil one picks us off, and our witness to the world is damaged.

And that brings us to the third point of Jesus's prayer. Why does He want us to walk in unity? By modeling a you-first life to a me-first world, we become His witnesses, "that the world may believe that You sent Me" (John 17:21). We are intended to shine for Him in a dark world. By our own choice and in our own strength, we will never walk in that higher calling. But as we are driven to depending upon God and one another, the Father will bring us into the unselfish unity for which His Son prayed. When that happens, we can walk as God has always desired His people to walk: modeling a sacrificial, you-first life to a me-first world, leading them away from the path that ends in death and onto the path that gives eternal life.

The Greatest Obstacle to Unity

As I mentioned in an earlier chapter, at the root of every sin is a broken relationship, either with God or with others. And at the root of every broken relationship is a hard heart. "Above all else, guard your heart, for it is the wellspring of life" (Proverbs 4:23 NIV). When we fail to guard our heart against hardness, life ceases to flow from us. And that is a very dangerous thing, as we see throughout the Bible.

In addition to the example of the prodigal's older brother, we have the classic example of Pharaoh. How many times do we read in Exodus of his hard heart?

If our heart is not right with God, we will not have any blessing for our neighbor.

And what was the final outcome for the Egyptian people? Although God used Pharaoh's hard heart to bring life to the people of Israel, the Egyptians paid a terrible price in the deaths of their firstborn sons. It was such a terrible price that each year, when the Jewish people observe Passover, they include in their oral remembrances the story of the sorrow experienced by their former captors.

Hard hearts negatively impact relationships because healthy, lasting, divinely ordained relationships depend on God's life within them to survive. If our heart is not right with God, we will not have any blessing for our neighbor. We will have nothing to give. Hard hearts are selfish hearts, and they always stand in the way of the unity God desires for us.

Mark 6:45–52 provides an excellent example of how God often deals with our hard hearts. This story occurs immediately following Jesus's miraculous feeding of the five thousand. Jesus sends His disciples across the lake, dismisses the crowd, and goes up the mountain to pray.

As a good friend of mine, pastor and author Duane Miller, always says, "God never does anything without a purpose." And, as Duane also points out, Jesus *made* the disciples go out onto the lake, and then He went off to pray. What was Jesus's purpose here? If we read on, we soon find the disciples caught in a terrible storm. Being experienced fishermen, perhaps they saw the storm coming and resisted Jesus's directions to get into the boat and go across to Bethsaida. But Jesus insisted, so off they went.

I believe Jesus purposely sent them out into the storm. Why did He do that? Look at verse 52: "For they had not understood about the loaves, because *their heart was hardened*" (emphasis added). Jesus allowed them to go through trial in order to soften their hearts for greater faith.

What the disciples could not learn from observing Jesus multiply the loaves and fish, they had to learn in the storm. As they struggled against the wind and waves, Jesus watched—and He prayed. I believe He was praying for the disciples, whom He was watching from afar. And when it was time (verse 48 says "about the fourth watch of the night," which is between 3:00 and 6:00 A.M.), He went to them, walking on the water.

> *And when they saw Him walking on the sea, they supposed it was a ghost, and cried out; for they all saw Him and were troubled. But immediately He talked with them and said to them, "Be of good cheer! It is I; do not be afraid."*
> *Then He went up into the boat to them, and the wind ceased. And they were greatly amazed in themselves beyond measure, and marveled.*
> *For **they had not understood about the loaves, because their heart was hardened.***
> —Mark 6:49–52 (emphasis added)

The disciples were no different from the rest of us. We seldom understand the things of God when we are witnessing a miracle. We enjoy those times, and we would all like to spend our time right there in the middle of the blessing. But it is only in the storms—in the midst of the tribulation that Jesus promised us—that our hard hearts begin to melt and to recognize just who this awesome, magnificent God really is.

I have another hero, whose name is Tyler Sexton. Tyler was born prematurely and was soon diagnosed with cerebral palsy. According to the medical experts, he had little chance of living to grow up, and if he did, he would never be out of a wheelchair. Tyler, who is now in his early 20s, walks with the aid of a service dog named Danny, who helps Tyler keep his balance. In addition, Tyler is a certified diver, has his driver's license, recently completed college, and is now attending medical school. A brilliant young man with a passion to tell others about how much he loves Jesus, he readily declares that he would not have achieved what he has today if God hadn't allowed him to go through some of the most difficult trials imaginable. As he says to the many young people he speaks to around the world, "I'd rather walk with a limp for Jesus than with a strut in the world."

> *"I'd rather walk with a limp for Jesus than with a strut in the world."*
> —Tyler Sexton

God can use suffering to stretch us and mature us. From another perspective, many in the persecuted church also understand that great growth can occur even in the midst of the storms of life. One particular believer, who ministers at great risk in Myanmar (Burma), is quoted in *The Voice of the Martyrs* magazine saying:

> *"We understand that discipleship and persecution go together. This is the path that Christ walked.... Don't pray that no problems may come. Pray that we will remain faithful to the Lord's work."*
> —THE VOICE OF THE MARTYRS, September 2006,
> www.persecution.com, Used by permission.

And so, Jesus admonishes us to "be of good cheer." The storms are coming, the tribulations are inevitable, but the purpose is to soften our hearts, open our understanding, and bring us to that unity that was the very heart cry of our beloved Savior in John 17—unity with God and with each other, even as the Father and Son are One.

By God's design, we need Him, and we need others. God's model for living requires that we be in relationships. If we are to bear much fruit in this life, we must depend on Him, "abide in

Him." And to abide in Him, we must guard our hearts and "walk just as He walked" (see 1 John 2:6), answering God's higher calling to live a you-first life for the sake of a needy, me-first world.

Making It Personal

1. What aspects of your life show that you haven't completely believed Jesus's statement that apart from Him you can do nothing? _____

_____

_____

_____

_____

_____

_____

_____

_____

_____

_____

2. Have you declared your independence from others? Or are you living your life in relationship with other Christian brothers and sisters? _____

_____

_____

_____

_____

_____

_____

_____

_____

_____

_____

3. When you consider that tribulation brings unity and strength to fulfill God's higher calling of modeling a you-first love to a me-first world, how does that change your attitude about experiencing trials and tribulations?

_____

_____

_____

_____

_____

_____

_____

_____

_____

4. Read John 15:1,4–5 and ask God to show you ways you've resisted letting go of your independence. Then pray and ask God to help you partner with other brothers and sisters in Christ to achieve the unity God wants us to experience. _____

_____

_____

_____

_____

_____

_____

_____

_____

_____

_____

9

Sealed for the Day

And do not grieve the Holy Spirit of God, by whom you were sealed for the day of redemption.
—Ephesians 4:30

No matter how many weddings I attend, whether they are for beloved family members, close friends, or casual acquaintances, I cry. When my youngest son, Chris, was united with his bride, Chasity, on a golden day in mid-October 1997, I cried. In fact, I nearly broke down. Then in September 2006, my middle son, Michael, took Risa to be his wife on a windswept beach in front of a small group of family and friends. I managed to hold myself together better on that occasion, maybe because we were all older by then, or maybe just because it was cold and I was too focused on keeping my teeth from chattering. In any case, both of these occasions are among the most precious and humbling moments of my life.

I know it's all right to cry. After all, a lot of people, particularly women, cry at weddings. But thinking more deeply about it, I realize the reason I cry is because I am overwhelmed. I am overwhelmed at the awesome nature of what is taking place. What a picture of God's yet-to-be-fulfilled promise to us, His bride. How thrilling to know with certainty that I, as part of the church, will one day participate in that heavenly ceremony, as our Bridegroom/Redeemer stands at our side and unites us to Himself forever.

In reality, of course, we are already united to Him. The bride-price has been paid, the offer of marriage made and accepted, and the token of betrothal given. We belong to Him, as surely as if the final ceremony had already taken place. And now we wait, preparing for and eagerly anticipating that wonderful day, when He will come for us, to take us to His Father's house, which He is readying for His bride.

The Marriage Covenant

Of course, the covenant of marriage was instituted by God Himself. Richard Booker, author of *Here Comes the Bride*, states that God gave to Israel "specific instructions for marriage in order to sanctify it properly as the basic unit of society." Booker continues: "He wanted to give marriage and family the permanency, protection and moral framework it needed for the good of society and the established social order.... God intended the marriage relationship to be permanent for the good of the couple and society as a whole."

> *Studying the beauty and depth of the ancient Jewish wedding can help us better understand both God's great love for us and the surety of His commitment to us.*

Studying the beauty and depth of the ancient Jewish wedding can help us better understand both God's great love for us and the surety of His commitment to us. The traditional wedding originally consisted of three phases: the arrangement phase (*shiddukhin*), the betrothal phase (*eyrusin*), and the marriage phase (*nissuin*).[1] The first phase of the Jewish wedding was known as the *shiddukhin* or arrangement period. In this phase, the preliminary arrangements are made. In ancient times these arrangements were sometimes made when the prospective bride and groom were still young children, even infants. Regardless of the age of the couple involved, these arrangements were usually made by the bridegroom's father or someone appointed by the father, called a *shadkhan*. A biblical example of this practice would be Abraham appointing his oldest servant to arrange for Isaac's marriage (to Rebekah) in Genesis 24. The one arranging the marriage must prepare and present a contract, specifying the terms of the marriage proposal, to the prospective bride and her father. Of the terms contained in the proposal, the bride-price or *mohar*—that which the prospective bridegroom was willing to pay the father for permission to marry his daughter—was the most important. If the father accepted the terms of the marriage contract, the decision was then up to his daughter. If she too accepted the terms of the proposal, the bridegroom would then deliver gifts to his bride, as a token of his love and a reminder of their future union.

In preparation for the second phase of the Jewish wedding, the betrothal phase or *eyrusin*, the bride and groom would each take a separate ceremonial cleansing bath (immersion or *mikveh*), signifying purification, in preparation for their future union. They would then appear under the *huppah* (wedding canopy) to share a cup of wine and publicly proclaim their betrothal. At that time, the couple was sanctified or set apart exclusively for each other, a significantly more serious circumstance than our modern-day engagement. This betrothal phase normally lasted for a period of one year, during which the couple was considered married but lived in separate dwellings.

Traditionally, and even in some modern Jewish weddings, the bride and groom each have specific duties to perform during the waiting period between betrothal and marriage. The bridegroom is busy preparing a dwelling place for himself and his bride, often an addition to his father's house. The bride concerns herself with the sewing of her wedding garments. She is also expected to set aside time for introspection and contemplation, in preparation for the completion of the marriage union.

The final phase, the *nissuin* (from the Hebrew word *nasa*, meaning "to carry"), was the marriage itself. Filled with anticipation, the bride never knew exactly when her groom would come "to carry" (*nasa*) her away to their new home. As a result, she had to be ready at all times. When the bridegroom, along with the wedding party, finally came for her, their arrival was announced only by a shout and the blowing of a *shofar* (ram's horn) before she was whisked away in the arms of her beloved. Once again, the couple would stand beneath the *huppah* and recite a blessing over a second cup of wine. This ceremony finalized their earlier proclamation of betrothal. The couple was now free to consummate their marriage and live together as husband and wife.

The Arrangements Have Been Made

The *shiddukhin*, or wedding arrangements, begin with the selection of the bride. Those of us who have received Jesus as our Savior have been chosen as His bride (see Ephesians 1:4). Our heavenly Father is the One who made that choice long ago. Think of it! We have been selected by God Himself to be the bride of His only Son. It is almost beyond our comprehension.

> *Think of it! We have been selected by God Himself to be the bride of His only Son.*

And then there is the bride-price, in this case, the death of the Sinless One. Jesus, the only One qualified to pay that price, willingly did so by giving His life for us. Our part, then, as summed up by the Apostle Paul in 1 Corinthians 6:19–20, is to give our life to Him in return:

> *Or do you not know that your body is the temple of the Holy Spirit who is in you, whom you have from God, and **you are not your own?** For **you were bought at a price;** therefore glorify God in your body and in your spirit, which are God's (emphasis added).*

Why is it so important to understand that the bride-price has already been paid for us and we no longer have claim to our lives? Paul, taking on the role of the *shadkhan* (the one who arranges a marriage at the direction of the groom's father), explained it clearly in 2 Corinthians 11:2: "For I have betrothed you to one husband, that I may present you as a chaste virgin to Christ."

Paul was writing to the church, trying to make them see that the arrangements had already been made, the price had been paid, and those who had received Jesus as Savior were now betrothed to the heavenly Bridegroom. Our responsibility, then, as those who have been set apart solely for Him, is to be faithful to Him as we anxiously await that great day when He will descend from heaven with a shout and the sounding of a *shofar* to carry us away to our new home.

A Pledge of His Love

According to ancient Jewish custom, once the bride has been chosen, the bride-price agreed upon and paid, and the proposal accepted by the bride, the groom gives some sort of gift, or token of betrothal, to his beloved to remind her of their future life together and to help her remain faithful to him as she awaits his coming. Jesus has given us such a token of betrothal: a pledge of His love and a reminder of the price He paid for us, as well as a promise that He will one day return to carry us away to our new home where we will live with Him forever. That gift is the Holy Spirit, received by each one who accepts the terms of the proposal offered to us by God. Jesus has gone to prepare a dwelling place for us, but He has promised to return, and in the meantime He has given a Gift to comfort and help us in His absence.

> *"Let not your heart be troubled; you believe in God, believe also in Me. In My Father's house are many mansions [permanent dwelling places]; if it were not so, I would have told you. I go to prepare a place for you. And if I go and prepare a place for you, I will come again and receive you to Myself; that where I am, there you may be also.... And I will pray the Father, and He will give you another Helper, that He may abide with you forever—the Spirit of truth, whom the world cannot receive, because it neither sees Him nor knows Him; but you know Him, for He dwells with you and will be in you. I will not leave you orphans; I will come to you.... It is to your advantage*

that I go away; for if I do not go away, the Helper will not come to you; but if I depart, I will send Him to you."
—John 14:1–3,16–18; 16:7

Jesus has given the Holy Spirit to us as a promise, a pledge, a seal to assure us that He will return for us. The Apostle Paul said in 2 Corinthians 1:22 that God "has sealed us and given us the Spirit in our hearts as a guarantee." A guarantee of what? That we have been chosen by God the Father and betrothed to God the Son, and that someday Jesus will return and carry us home. Paul reiterates that thought in Ephesians 1:13, where he writes that we have been "sealed with the Holy Spirit of promise," and again in Ephesians 4:30, where he says that we have been "sealed for the day of redemption," the day of our Bridegroom's return.

Jesus knew it would be a long time before He finished His preparations and came back for us; He also knew we would begin to wonder if He had forgotten about us or stopped loving us. Therefore, one of the purposes of the gift of the Holy Spirit is to "[bear] witness with our spirit that we are children of God, and if children, then heirs—heirs of God and joint heirs with Christ" (Romans 8:16–17). Our Bridegroom has sent us a wonderful gift to bear witness with our spirit, to remind us of His love for and commitment to us. But His gift to us is more than just a reminder; the Holy Spirit has been given to us to enable us to prepare ourselves to be that "chaste virgin" (2 Corinthians 11:2), that sanctified bride and glorious church without "spot or wrinkle or any such thing...holy and without blemish" (Ephesians 5:27), that our beloved Bridegroom so richly deserves.

> *A guarantee of what? That we have been chosen by God the Father and betrothed to God the Son, and that someday Jesus will return and carry us home.*

We Are Now Betrothed

The bride of Christ is now in the betrothal, or *eyrusin,* phase in relation to her heavenly Bridegroom. It is, as I've said, a much more serious and permanent phase of relationship than our modern engagement period, which is so often and easily broken. In ancient Israel, once a couple had entered into the betrothal phase of marriage, the relationship could not be ended except by obtaining a *get*, the equivalent of a religious divorce, and that option was open only to the husband, not the wife. Once we are betrothed to Jesus, the relationship is to be permanent; we have no legal right to end it.

This is the situation that Mary and Joseph were in when the angel Gabriel appeared to the young maiden to tell her of the great honor to be bestowed upon her.

> *Now in the sixth month the angel Gabriel was sent by God to a city of Galilee named Nazareth, to a virgin **betrothed** to a man whose name was Joseph, of the house of David. The virgin's name was Mary....*
> *Then the angel said to her, "Do not be afraid, Mary, for you have found favor with God. "And behold, you will conceive in your womb and bring forth a Son, and shall call His name JESUS."*
> —Luke 1:26–27,30–31 (emphasis added)

For a young girl, betrothed to be married but not yet living with her husband, this was an awkward situation, to say the least— particularly in a time when infidelity could have been punished by stoning. But when we look at the story in the Gospel of Matthew, we see that Joseph, although a just and righteous man, was also a man of mercy and compassion.

> *Now the birth of Jesus Christ was as follows: After His mother Mary was betrothed to Joseph, before they came together, she was found with child of the Holy Spirit. Then Joseph her husband, being a just man, and not wanting to make her a public example, was minded to put her away secretly.*
> —Matthew 1:18–19

Although by Jewish law Joseph, when he learned of Mary's pregnancy, had the right to publicly expose her and have her stoned to death, he instead planned to "put her away secretly," or obtain a *get*, a divorce. Of course, it never came to that because God revealed to Joseph in a dream that Mary had not been unfaithful, that she was pregnant "of the Holy Spirit" (v. 20), and that he should go ahead with his plans to marry her.

The seriousness of the betrothal relationship is evidenced in this illustration of Joseph and Mary. And it is in that same stage of relationship that we now find ourselves as the bride of Christ—betrothed, with Holy Spirit life inside us, waiting for the second coming of Jesus, even as Mary awaited His first coming. And just as surely as He came that first time, He will come again for us.

A Time of Preparation

Because we, as the bride of Christ, are in the betrothal period, we are also in a time of preparation. And as the return of our Bridegroom draws breathtakingly near, the pace of preparation intensifies. As the bride in the ancient Jewish wedding used the betrothal time to sew her wedding garment, so our garment must be made ready as well. That garment must be a garment of purity, without spot, wrinkle, or blemish. Yet do we have the ability to clean or iron that wedding garment ourselves? Absolutely not. God, in Isaiah 64:6, declared our own efforts at purity and righteousness to be "like filthy rags." So how are we to prepare?

We prepare by realizing that we cannot prepare on our own. We can do nothing, in and of ourselves, to make ourselves worthy to come into the presence of a holy God, let alone be joined to Him in marriage. Even as I recognized so many years ago in that Catholic convent, there is absolutely nothing I can do—then or ever—to make myself worthy to come into His presence.

Yet God has called us to be holy even as He is holy (see Leviticus 11:44–45). He has, in essence, called us to the impossible. The only hope we have is to throw ourselves at His feet and cry out, "I can't do it, Lord! Help me. Make me the person you want me to be."

Ah, music to God's ears! Just the words He longs to hear from each of us. It is a truth He has always known, a truth many of us claim to know but fail to exhibit by our actions. Jesus told us that without Him we could do nothing. And nothing means nothing—including making ourselves holy. The prophet Jeremiah framed this dilemma so eloquently when he wrote, "Can the Ethiopian change his skin or the leopard its spots? Then may you also do good who are accustomed to do evil" (Jeremiah 13:23).

What God, through Jeremiah, was saying is this: When a leopard can, in and of its own ability, change its coat from spotted to striped, then sinners will be able to turn themselves into saints. And we all know that is never going to happen.

So how are we to obey God's command to be holy as He is holy? By admitting that we can never change ourselves by ourselves, and appealing to God's Spirit within us—the token of our betrothal to Him—to do the work. As surely as it was God's Spirit that wooed us, convicted us, and brought new life to us when we were born again, it is God, through the working of His Spirit, who is now in the process of completing the good work in us.

He who has begun a good work in you will complete it until the day of Jesus Christ.
—Philippians 1:6

But we all, with unveiled face, beholding as in a mirror the glory of the Lord, are being transformed into the same image from glory to glory, just as by the Spirit of the Lord.
—2 Corinthians 3:18

The Lord will perfect that which concerns me; Your mercy, O Lord, endures forever; Do not forsake the works of Your hands.
—Psalm 138:8

God, at the point of our rebirth, began a good work in us, and He has promised to complete that good work by transforming us from the image of our first fallen ancestor, Adam, to the image of our Bridegroom, Jesus Christ. God Himself will wash out the spots and blemishes, iron out the wrinkles, and present us to His Son "a chaste virgin," worthy to be eternally united with the King of kings and Lord of lords.

Our relationships with God and with others rub off our rough edges and transform us from the selfish, me-first beings that we are to the unselfish, you-first bride that God wants us to become.

That's what this betrothal period is all about. God has already chosen and redeemed us. We have been "bought with a price," and we belong to Him because He gave Himself for us. Now it is His purpose to change us, and not just individually but corporately, into the bride with whom He longs to spend eternity.

So how does God's Spirit within us accomplish that change? Primarily through relationships. Although God also uses circumstances in our changing process, they are a secondary element in the equation. Our relationships with God and with others rub off our rough edges and transform us from the selfish, me-first beings that we are to the unselfish, you-first bride that God wants us to become.

I wrote in the last chapter about God's use of tribulation to press or merge us into unity with others, to bring us to a place where we are one, even as the Father and Son are one. And yet, tribulation is nothing more than trying circumstances. Tribulation or adverse circumstances don't change us—the relationships those circumstances press us into do.

The old saying that tragedy and suffering can make us bitter or better is a very true statement, so far as it encompasses relationships. We have a choice. And it is the choice that will define how well we prepare for our returning Bridegroom. When we go through trials, we can choose to harden our hearts against God and others, allowing a root of bitterness to take hold and grow until it chokes the very life out of us. Or we can choose to yield ourselves to the changes God wants to make in us, which means learning to depend on Him and on others, putting God's will and other people's needs above our own. In other words, living a you-first life in a me-first world. And that is no small order.

Living for God and for others will require change. Change frightens us—and we don't like to be frightened. Change hurts—and we don't like to be hurt. Change will require giving up certain comforts and conveniences. No wonder we fight it with such tenacity!

Nevertheless, there truly is no other way to be holy, to be godly, to walk as He has called us to walk, to be transformed into His image. God sent His Spirit as a token of our betrothal, to remind us of our binding commitment to Him. Because of His work in our lives, we can choose to live for Him instead of ourselves. And living for Him today will prepare us for the coming day when He returns to take us home.

Time to Grow Up in Unity and Love

The betrothal period is a time of maturing. As a young woman and a young man prepare for the adult responsibilities of marriage and maintaining a household during engagement, we too are expected to mature in the faith, to grow up. In this betrothal period the Holy Spirit is molding and shaping us, changing us from spoiled children

> *Because of His work in our lives, we can choose to live for Him instead of ourselves.*

who demand our own way into mature sons and daughters, eager to serve Him and others. The Apostle Paul expresses it so well in his letter to the Ephesians:

> *Till we all come to the unity of the faith and of the knowledge of the Son of God, to a perfect man, to the measure of the stature of the fullness of Christ; that we should no longer be children, tossed to and fro and carried about with every wind of doctrine, by the trickery*

*of men, in the cunning craftiness of deceitful plotting,
but, speaking the truth in love, may grow up in all things
into Him who is the head—Christ—from whom the
whole body, joined and knit together by what every joint
supplies, according to the effective working by which
every part does its share, causes growth of the body for
the edifying of itself in love.*
—Ephesians 4:13–16

We will never grow up through the mere amassing of biblical knowledge, the mastery of powerful prayer formulas, or the respectability of our lifestyle. We will only grow up when we can say, like John the Baptist, "He must increase, but I must decrease" (John 3:30). In other words, we must lay aside our own dreams, our own desires, our own plans, in essence, our own kingdoms, and dedicate ourselves to fulfilling *His* dreams, *His* desires, *His* plans, for *His* kingdom.

Brothers and sisters, it is time to grow up. We've got to put aside our childish ways. God's desire is for us to walk in love for Him, for each other (the church) and for the world. Let's leave behind the selfishness, the quarrels, the bickering, the pettiness, the unhealthy divisions. Let us strive for the unity in this beautiful Psalm:

*Behold, how good and how pleasant it is for brethren to
dwell in unity!
It is like the precious oil upon the head, running down on
the beard, the beard of Aaron, running down on the edge
of his garments.
It is like the dew of Hermon, descending upon the
mountains of Zion; For there the Lord commanded the
blessing—Life forevermore.*
—Psalm 133:1–3

If we are to be one in God and if the world is to know Jesus is God's Son (John 17:21), then we must move beyond words. Oh, we've talked a lot about walking in selfless, unconditional love, but with few exceptions, we haven't modeled it—nor will we, so long as we insist on doing things *our* way, in *our* time, for *our* own benefit. But when we begin to lay down our lives for others, willingly placing others' needs above our own, the world will sit up and take notice. Of course, as I wrote in an earlier chapter, not everyone will suddenly become a Christian. But the difference between the believers and the rest of the world will be undeniable. Then, whether or not the lost repent and turn their lives over to God, they will have been convicted, and they will be without excuse when they stand before the Judge of the universe.

[1] There are many variations on the Jewish wedding ceremony. Not all teachings match the one described in this chapter. The author would like to acknowledge that Barney Kasdan's book *God's Appointed Customs* was particularly helpful to her in understanding the background of the Jewish wedding. See especially "The Jewish Wedding," p. 47–70.

God's Appointed Customs, copyright© 1996 by Barney Kasdan. Published by Messianic Jewish Publishers, 6120 Day Long Lane, Clarksville, Maryland 20129. www.messianicjewish.net

Making It Personal

1. How does understanding the betrothal period in ancient Jewish custom change your sense of belonging and permanence in your relationship to Christ? _____

_____

_____

_____

_____

_____

_____

_____

_____

_____

_____

2. Understanding that as part of the bride of Christ you are now in the betrothal or preparation period, what areas of your life might you want to reprioritize, and why?

_____

_____

_____

_____

_____

_____

_____

_____

_____

_____

3. If you begin to think of the Holy Spirit as a promise from your heavenly Bridegroom, how might that change the way you respond to the Spirit's promptings? _____

_____

_____

_____

_____

_____

_____

_____

_____

_____

_____

_____

_____

4. Read Ephesians 4:30 and ask God to show you if there are times you have grieved the Holy Spirit. Then ask Him to forgive you and to make your heart tender toward Him.

_____

_____

_____

_____

_____

_____

_____

_____

_____

_____

_____

_____

_____

10

"Do You Love Me More Than These?"

So when they had eaten breakfast, Jesus said to Simon Peter, "Simon, son of Jonah, do you love Me more than these?" He said to Him, "Yes, Lord, You know that I love You." He said to him, "Feed My lambs."
—John 21:15

Several years ago my life was jolted from its somewhat predictable routine by an event that, for me, challenged everything I have written in this book. It was late on Easter night. The phone rang. I fumbled for the receiver and heard my daughter-in-law Christy say, "Mom? I'm sorry to wake you, but—"

"Is everything all right?" I interrupted, as all sorts of horrible images flashed through my mind. *Was it Michael? One of the kids?*

"What happened?" I asked, gripping the phone as if it would keep me from falling into some fearsome black hole.

"It's Mike," she said, confirming one of my worst fears. "He's been in an accident. His neck is...broken."

As her story unfolded, I learned that, a few hours earlier, my middle son had been riding a dirt bike in the desert, not far from where they lived. He'd been riding for years. I knew he was careful and responsible, that he always wore a helmet—facts Christy confirmed—but something had gone wrong with the gears on the bike. In the middle of a jump, the bike lost power and dropped

Michael onto his head, crushing four of the seven vertebrae in his neck. He also had bleeding on his brain and multiple skull fractures. The prognosis was not good.

I managed to hold myself together until I hung up the phone, knowing Christy did not need to deal with my hysteria on top of everything else. But once the receiver was back on the hook, I fell apart, sobbing, even as I struggled to find the words to pray.

Suddenly, I was faced with some very serious questions. Did I really believe what I claimed to believe, or was it all just fancy words, designed to paint a compelling picture that no one, including myself, would ever live up to? Was walking as God has called us to walk, living a you-first life in a me-first world, an impossible ideal? Or was it, as I have maintained throughout the writing of this book, the only true path to ultimate joy and fulfillment? If so, did I want to follow my Savior's model badly enough to give up everything else to walk it?

To say it was a long night would be an understatement. So many plans and arrangements had to be made—airline reservations from Portland to Los Angeles, phone calls, packing, canceling and rescheduling appointments. But by the time I finally stood beside my son's hospital bed, stroking his arm and whispering his name, the question of choosing God's way over my own had already been settled. For sometime during that long dark night, God had confronted me with the words, "Give Michael to Me."

"What do you mean, God?" I had protested. "He's already Yours. I gave him to You a long time ago. I know You'll take care of him now."

But deep down, I knew that was not what God was saying. He wanted me to give my son to Him *unconditionally*, not with the provision to heal him and take care of him, but a total release of him for whatever God's purposes might be. I knew He was saying that, but I did not want to hear it. Then the Lord brought a Scripture to my mind:

"He who loves father or mother more than Me is not worthy of Me. And he who loves son or daughter more

than Me is not worthy of Me. And he who does not take his cross and follow after Me is not worthy of Me."
—Matthew 10:37–38

God wasn't saying that I should stop loving or being concerned about my son. He was challenging me to check my heart, to see if He was still in first place, to see if I truly loved Him more than anything or anyone else, even my children. To whom would I cling in this moment of testing—my beloved son or my faithful Father? *Whom did I love more?*

In that valley of decision, I suddenly remembered what God had said to me so many years earlier: Your sin was not in the things you did, nor was it in loving other things or other people too much. Your sin was in not loving Me enough.

I reached up to God and, with an aching heart, laid my son at His feet, with no conditions, no requirements, no bargaining, only the knowledge that God is always right and that I can trust Him, no matter what lies ahead, no matter what happens.

My heart soared as I sensed the peaceful presence of a perfect and holy God in the midst of a terrifying situation. And I knew I had made the right choice—the only choice. Not only had I acknowledged my own inability to care for my son and wisely placed him in the hands of the only One who could, I had also acknowledged God's sovereignty over all that I am, all that I love and hold dear. I had answered His question of "Do you love Me more than these?" The answer was yes.

Your sin was in not loving Me enough.

Miraculously, Michael was home from the hospital a week later, walking with the aid of a walker and sporting a halo bolted into his skull, which he would have to wear for several months. Though he still had a long rehabilitation period ahead of him, the doctors agreed it would be a full recovery, and they were right.

What a testimony to God's faithfulness!

However, I can say without hesitation that, had Michael not survived this accident or had he ended up in a wheelchair, God would be no less faithful. I would still have made the right choice to yield my desires for my son's life to the only One who has a rightful claim on that life. It wasn't that I stopped praying for God's healing; it was that my focus shifted from my desires to God's, even as my faith shifted from God's promises to God Himself. *For our faith can never be in what God does for us, but rather, in God Himself.*

"Follow Me"

"Do you love me more than these?"

Jesus, after His resurrection, confronted Peter with that very question. He confronts each of His followers with that question in different ways. It is a question that, ultimately, each of us must answer in the affirmative if we are to be effective in modeling a Christ-like lifestyle. And it is a question that will cut to the very heart of our identity, challenging both our love and our loyalty.

When Jesus confronted Peter with that question of first love and first loyalty in John 21, it was a pivotal time for the rugged-fisherman-turned-apostle. I have to believe that when Jesus first asked the question Peter couldn't help but remember how recently he had declared his loyalty and dedication to Jesus, only to later fail miserably and deny Him three times. Although Jesus and Peter were not speaking Greek during this exchange, the Greek equivalent for the word Jesus used for love in that verse (15) is the word *agapaō*, denoting "to love (in a social or moral sense)," according to Strong's Concordance. Peter, on the other hand, answered, "Yes, Lord; You know that I love you" (v. 15), using the equivalent of the Greek word *phileō* to describe his love. *Phileō* love means to "be fond of or feel friendly and affectionate toward." Strong's explains the difference in this way: "[*Agapaō*] is wider [than *phileō*], embracing especially the judgment and deliberate assent of the will as a matter of principle, duty and propriety."

It seems that Peter, having so recently come face to face with his own weakness, was unwilling to commit to more than an affectionate feeling toward Jesus. Graciously, Jesus did not comment on Peter's substitution of words; rather, He gave him a directive: "Feed My lambs" (v. 15). He then repeated His question: "Simon, son of Jonah, do you love [*agapaō*] Me?" (v. 16). Peter answered the same way he had the first time. Then Jesus said, "Tend My sheep" (v. 16).

Finally, Jesus asked, "Simon, son of Jonah, do you love [*phileō*] Me?" (v. 17). This time the Savior used the lesser meaning of love in His question, as if bringing the question of Peter's loyalty to a level the fisherman could understand. Yet Peter was grieved because Jesus had to ask him this question three times. How heavy Peter's heart must have been as his recent failure weighed upon his broad shoulders.

"Lord, You know all things," he responded. "You know that I love You."

"Feed My sheep," Jesus said (v. 17).

The beautiful thing about this conversation between the risen Lord and His follower is that Jesus did not mention Peter's terrible failure. He didn't admonish him, correct him, or chastise him. He simply repeated His question and directive in such a way as to bring Peter's focus back to what is most important:

> "'*You shall love the* LORD *your God with all your heart, with all your soul, and with all your mind.' This is the first and great commandment. And the second is like it: 'You shall love your neighbor as yourself.' On these two commandments hang all the Law and the Prophets.*"
> —Matthew 22:37–40

"Do you love Me *more than these*?" In essence, Jesus was saying to His disciple, Am I first in your heart, Peter? Do you love Me with all your heart, soul, mind, and strength? Then give your life away, as I have done, to show your love for your neighbor. Feed My flock, tend them, lead them, guide them, teach them. Out of your love for Me, minister to others. Fulfill My higher calling on your life, Peter. Forget about yourself—your clay feet, your weak will, your faults and failures. Just concentrate on loving Me and putting others ahead of yourself. That is My higher calling to you: to go beyond yourself and model a you-first love in a me-first world.

What is God's higher calling but a call to follow His Son, to walk as He walked, to love as He loved, to give as He gave? Jesus acknowledged that His sole purpose here on earth was to accomplish the Father's will, as He so clearly stated in the Garden of Gethsemane: "Nevertheless, not as I will, but as You will" (Matthew 26:39). If we are to follow in His footsteps, then we must dedicate our lives to that same purpose.

The message of the Savior to His disciple was: It will cost you everything, Peter. *Everything*. The strength and independence of your past life is over. The only strength you will now have will be found in your love for and dependence upon Me. But out of that strength you will gladly lay down your life for the gospel, as you tend and feed my sheep (see John 21:18–19).

And then Jesus summed up His directive to Peter with two simple words: "Follow Me" (John 21:19).

"What About Him?"

Poor Peter. A simple fisherman who had spent his entire life depending on his own strength and skill now found himself being challenged to do the impossible: to follow in the footsteps of the holy, sinless Son of God, the One he had so recently denied. Can't you just imagine his dilemma? No one knew better than Peter his inability to fulfill that directive. Yet, because he truly did love Jesus and want to follow Him, he found himself in a very difficult position indeed. He was not about to say no to his Lord, but he did not want to make a promise he could not keep. And so, like the rest of us, he searched for an excuse.

Glancing around, Peter saw John, the Beloved Apostle. "What about him?" he asked Jesus. Maybe Peter's thinking went like this: *You've given me an overwhelming assignment. You're not going to let him off without something equally daunting, are You? Aren't You going to require the same of him as You have of me?* (See John 21:20–21.) But Jesus's answer did not let Peter off the hook. If anything, it denied him his last excuse.

Jesus said to him, "If I will that he remain till I come, what is that to you? *You follow Me*" (v. 22, emphasis added). Those words speak volumes to all of us, don't they? How inept we feel when we receive an assignment from God! And how quickly we look around at others and whine, "But, God, why do I have to do that? I don't see anybody else doing it. Why me? Why not them?"

At that point, if we are honest and have "ears to hear," we will have our answer: *What is that to you? You follow Me.*

There really is no way around it, is there? If we have received Jesus as Savior, we are called to walk as He walked, just as God has called His people to walk throughout the centuries. We are to model a you-first life to a me-first world, loving God first and then giving of ourselves to strengthen our fellow believers and to draw unbelievers to Him.

Without God's Spirit within us, we can't do it. Without His sustaining grace and strength, we're doomed to failure. He wants us to depend on Him alone. So long as we think we can wash out our own spots and iron out our own wrinkles, we will never answer God's higher calling: to walk as Jesus walked, doing only those things He saw the Father do, and doing it all by the power of the Holy Spirit, by whom we have been "sealed for the day of redemption" (Ephesians 4:30).

For we are betrothed to Christ, remember? He is coming back for us! And while He is gone, He has given us His Spirit as a token, a reminder of our betrothal and of His soon-coming return. It is that very Spirit living within us that will do the necessary work to prepare us for that glorious day.

Our part is to guard our hearts, to keep them soft and vulnerable and receptive to His voice, and to cultivate our love for Him and for others.

Our part is to guard our hearts, to keep them soft and vulnerable and receptive to His voice, and to cultivate our love for Him and for others. In doing so, we are fulfilling the greatest commandments, the two commandments upon which hang "all the Law and the Prophets": to love God with all our heart, mind, soul, and strength...and our neighbor as ourselves.

Grateful to Be a Part of This

Years ago, when I was actively involved in jail and prison ministry through our church, I always found it interesting to talk with others about how they got into that particular type of service. A single mom I'll call Barbara seemed especially dedicated to ministering behind bars, and one day I had a chance to ask her about it.

Her smile was immediate, as her blue eyes lit up and she readily shared her story. "I got involved in prison ministry about four years ago," she said. "And I absolutely love it. These people are, after all, our neighbors, and Jesus told us to love them, which I do! But the story behind it..." Her smile faded then, and she glanced down before looking up and continuing. A sadness had dulled the light in her eyes.

"I was 19," she said. "I had just moved out on my own, but I was still very close to my parents and my teenage brother, Richard. I visited them several times a week and talked with my mom on the phone almost daily. One weekend Richard came over to spend the weekend with me in my little apartment. We talked to our parents on Saturday evening, and all was fine. But Sunday afternoon, when I gave Richard a ride home, we knew something was wrong.

"My parents were 'neatniks,' creatures of habit. The first thing they did in the morning was open the front drapes and bring in the newspaper. When my brother and I got to their house, the drapes were still drawn and the paper was still in the driveway. Slowly we made our way to the back door, which was always unlocked. When we eased it open, my mom's poodle made a beeline past us and raced away down the street. I looked at Richard, terrified, and then we stepped inside."

Tears had formed in her eyes by then, and one escaped and slid down her cheek. I knew what she was going to say, and I wanted to beg her not to—but she did.

"My parents were...dead. Murdered in their bed. What little cash and jewelry they'd had in the house was gone. And my brother and I were the ones who found their bodies."

I swallowed, barely able to speak. "I'm so sorry, Barbara," I said. "I had no idea. Did they catch the people who did it?"

She nodded. "Yes, and he's serving a sentence of life without parole." Her face brightened slightly and she wiped away her tears. "In fact, he's the reason I'm here."

I frowned, puzzled. "What do you mean?"

"My brother and I were so devastated by the murder of our parents and then finding their bodies that we both went into a bit of a tailspin, I'm afraid. Richard seemed to get over it and get on with his life better than I did, but I just couldn't get those images of my parents out of my mind. I found myself growing vengeful and thinking I would feel better if the person who did it paid with his own life.

"When the guy was arrested, I went to the trial every day, determined to see him found guilty and get the death penalty. But something else was going on in my life at that time. I had met a lady at work who was constantly talking to me about Jesus and telling me she was praying for me. One day, when she walked by my desk, I asked her if she was still praying for me. I don't even know why I said that; I hadn't planned to. But she turned to me and said, 'Of course, I am. Would you like me to pray for you right now?' We walked to the break room together, while I kept asking myself why I was going with her. But for some reason, I just couldn't seem to stop. When we found the break room empty, she looked at me and said, 'Is there anything special you want me to pray for?' Without any intention of doing so, I began to cry and told her how I was feeling about losing my parents and about the man who did it and how I wondered if I would ever be able to get over it.

"We sat together on a small couch, and she held me while I cried. When my sobs had subsided, she began to pray for God's mercy and love and peace to flow through me—and I could feel it! I had never experienced anything like it before. Then she began to tell me how God loved me so much that He had sent His only Son,

Jesus, to die for my sins and to reunite me to my heavenly Father. When she asked if I wanted to pray to receive Jesus as my Savior, I said yes, and...well, the rest is history, I suppose."

By then she was beaming again, and my heart was soaring too. What a wonderful salvation story! But how did that explain her involvement in prison ministry?

Barbara must have sensed my confusion because she continued. "As the trial for my parents' accused killer continued, I found my desire for revenge lessening, and I began to see him as another sinner who needed God's grace and forgiveness, just like me. And so, I began to pray for him—not only that he would recognize his need for salvation but also that he wouldn't get the death penalty.

> *"Isn't that amazing? The man who was a murderer is now a new creature in Christ—my brother in the Lord."*
> *—Barbara*

When he was convicted and given a life sentence, I wrote him a letter telling him I had forgiven him and was praying for him to come to know Jesus as I did. We still correspond in letters, and a couple of years ago he wrote to tell me that he had accepted Jesus as his Savior.

"Isn't that amazing? The man who was a murderer is now a new creature in Christ, my brother in the Lord. The more I thought about that, the more I knew God was calling me to tell others behind bars about the love and forgiveness of Jesus. So...here I am! God has melted all the hard places in my heart and given me a love for these inmates that could only come from Him. And I'm so grateful to be a part of this."

Indeed. As am I, Barbara. As am I.

Isn't it amazing that the Father has given us new hearts—hearts of flesh—that beat in tune with His and love unconditionally? That's what makes us family. And that's what unites us in a common purpose—to go into all the world and make disciples, completing the ministry of reconciliation by living a you-first life in a me-first world.

Remember the verse that began the introduction to this book? "Above all else, guard your heart, for it is the wellspring of life"

(Proverbs 4:23 NIV). It is a verse worth memorizing and living out on a daily basis. May that wellspring of life flow from our tender hearts to the lambs and sheep we have been commissioned to tend and feed. And may we live following our Savior, who willingly laid down His life for us, and our Father, who gave His only Son so that we prodigals could be welcomed home.

Making It Personal

1. Describe a difficult situation in your own life where you had to make a choice to yield to God unconditionally. What was the outcome? _____

_____

_____

_____

_____

_____

_____

_____

_____

_____

2. Consider how Peter felt when asked by Jesus—whom he had recently denied three times—if he loved Him "more than these." Now describe a situation where you too failed or denied Jesus, only to be confronted soon after by the question of your love for Him. How did it make you feel? How did you respond? _____

_____

_____

_____

_____

_____

_____

_____

_____

_____

3. Think of a time when God called you to do something that seemed impossible and you found yourself, like Peter, looking for a way to shift the focus from yourself to someone else? What was the outcome? _____

_____

_____

_____

_____

_____

_____

_____

_____

_____

_____

_____

4. Read John 21:15 and ask God to show you how you could better feed God's lambs by loving Him more. _____

_____

_____

_____

_____

_____

_____

_____

_____

_____

_____

_____

_____

_____

Appendix
Dad and Me

"Assuredly, I say to you, whoever does not receive the kingdom of God as a little child will by no means enter it."
—Mark 10:15

My dad was my first hero. I loved him and looked up to him in every possible way—except one. He claimed to be an atheist, and I simply couldn't accept that. Even though I didn't come to know God until my mid-20s, I always believed God existed. I could never really figure out why my dad didn't, especially since he'd had a Christian mother who had prayed for him for years.

My paternal grandmother, "Omi," was a tiny little German woman with a very big heart. Orphaned before age ten, she was sent to live on a dairy farm with a Lutheran pastor's family. Omi worked hard to earn her keep, but she also learned from them the joy of knowing Jesus—"Yesus" she called Him. Years later, in her 70s and 80s, she often laid her hand on her chest and said, "I have my Yesus in my heart."

Omi married just before the outbreak of World War I. When her husband went to fight in the Kaiser's army, Omi was left to care for my dad and his little brother. That little brother died of malnutrition before war's end, and Dad spent weeks in a government-run hospital, suffering from scurvy, a vitamin C deficiency. Omi sat at his bedside, praying and singing hymns in German, assuring him that Jesus loved him. The hungry little boy, miserable from the illness that plagued him, found that hard to believe.

Life improved after the war ended and my grandfather returned. Two more sons and a daughter were added to the family. When my dad reached his eighteenth birthday, it was time to go out and make his own way in life.

He arrived in America in 1929, just as the Depression started. His hopes of a better life seemed dashed. Nevertheless he struggled through, working as a *vaquero* (cowboy) on a large cattle ranch. Though he had few possessions, he was getting two meals a day, more than many other people at that time.

Gradually things improved, and Dad's life was looking up. Then came the Second World War. His family, still in Germany, suffered through the chaos and horror of that time, losing one son and nearly another. The war finally ended, and a few years later Dad brought his parents and remaining siblings to the United States to start a new life.

My father had married my mother by this time, and we three children soon followed. Still Dad refused to believe in God. Then in 1969, Bob, my 19-year-old brother, went to church with his boss one Sunday and received Jesus as his Savior. Soon off to Bible college, Bob prayed diligently for the rest of us. Omi, of course, was praying right along with him.

Mom was the next to become a Christian, in 1970, followed in 1971 by my other brother, Jerry. Dad and I were the only holdouts. I hardened my heart. Even though I was no atheist, I didn't see any reason to go to church every Sunday and carry a big Bible around all the time. After all, I was a good person... wasn't I?

Then, on July 2, 1974, my mom's fifty-third birthday, she awoke with an assurance in her heart that could only come from God Himself. She knew He was calling her to pray for my salvation and that I was going to respond quickly. At the time, however, I was more than 1,000 miles away, living in another state.

My mother and two faithful friends prayed urgently for my salvation over the next few days. At the same time, though far away, my heart began to feel torn in two. Finally, on July 5, I called my mom. Her only response was, "You need Jesus."

That wasn't what I'd hoped to hear, so I cut the call short. But just before I hung up, Mom made me promise that when I got off the phone I would pray. I agreed but quickly forgot.

Nevertheless, I became aware of a strange sensation—I felt dirty. I tried to dismiss it, but it wouldn't go away. So I stopped what I was doing and took a shower. It didn't help. I still felt dirty, and that's when I realized the problem was on the inside. (Romans 3:23 says: "For all have sinned and fall short of the glory of God" [NIV].)

Remembering my promise to my mother, I dropped to my knees beside my bed and began to pray: "Jesus, I don't know if I'm saying this right or even exactly what it means, but I know I need You. I'm so sorry for all the things I've done, all the people I've hurt, the way I've turned my back on You for so many years. Please forgive me, and come into my heart. Be my Savior and my Lord."

For me, on that very day, everything changed. Joy and peace washed over me in waves. I realized I had to rethink everything, sifted through the new, tender heart God had given me. And I couldn't wait to tell everyone how wonderful it was to have "Yesus" in my heart!

Omi died the next year, rejoicing that most of her family had come to know Jesus as she did. Nonetheless, Dad continued to harden his heart and refused to believe—until just after his eighty-eighth birthday, when a series of health problems took their toll.

Less than a week before his death, Dad seemed to return to his boyhood days in a German hospital, listening to his mother pray and sing to him in German. Then he himself began to sing those old German hymns about "Yesus." As I wept with joy, he switched to English and sang, "Jesus loves me, this I know, for the Bible tells me so."

From that point on, at the mention of the name of Jesus, Dad lit up like a Christmas tree, lifting his right hand and pointing heavenward, grinning and gesturing, even though he could no longer speak. His final days were filled with joy, and we were able to let him go, knowing he was at peace with God.

Yes, my first hero is waiting for me in heaven, and I am so very grateful. But isn't it sad that he hardened his heart for so many years and missed the joy of serving our wonderful Savior here on earth! The Bible says: "There is only one Lord, and he is generous to everyone who asks for his help. All who call out to the Lord will be saved" (Romans 10:12–13 CEV). If you want to know peace with God, to receive a new heart made to love Him and your neighbor, may I encourage you to pray now? God tells us: "For the wages of sin is death, but the gift of God is eternal life in Christ Jesus our Lord" (Romans 6:23 NIV).

Pray this simple prayer—tell God in your own words that you want to follow and trust Him as a little child is led by his or her parents; a wonderful journey of faith and obedience awaits you.

Dear God, thank You for loving me so much that You sent Your only Son, Jesus, to die for me. I believe He rose from the dead and is alive today. Forgive me for all my sins and for leaving You out of my life all these years. Please send Your Holy Spirit to live in my heart now, to change me, and to give me the assurance that I will spend eternity in heaven with You. I want to follow you, loving you and loving my neighbor. I ask it in Jesus's name. Amen.

If you prayed this prayer, or if you'd just like to drop me a note, please stop by my Web site, www.kathimacias.com, and send me an email or sign my guest book. I'd love to hear from you!

New Hope® Publishers is a division of WMU®, an international organization that challenges Christian believers to understand and be radically involved in God's mission. For more information about WMU, go to www.wmu.com. Visit newhopepublishers.com for more information about New Hope books. New Hope books may be purchased at your local bookstore.